The Intricacies of Small-Scale Business

Elvis Gbodi Ajai

Copyright © 2024 Elvis Gbodi Ajai

The Intricacies of Small-Scale Business. All rights reserved

All rights reserved. No part of this publication may be reproduced, transmitted, or stored in a retrieval system in any form or by any means, without permission in writing from the copyright holder.

ISBN 978-8-3985-7042-8

CHAPTER ONE

DEFINING WHAT A BUSINESS TRULY IS

When most people hear the word "business," they often picture cash registers ringing, online sales notifications pinging, or perhaps a street vendor shouting prices over the din of a busy marketplace. This surface-level understanding is not uncommon especially in small-scale enterprises, where the day-to-day hustle can easily mask the broader picture. But while buying and selling may be central activities, they are not what truly define a business.

To grasp the essence of a business, particularly one designed for sustainable success and growth, we must move beyond this narrow view. At its core, a business is not just an exchange of goods or services for money. It is a deliberately structured system designed to deliver consistent value to a target audience in a way that is scalable, profitable, and sustainable over time. Understanding this distinction is critical for anyone seeking to transition from a transactional mindset into a strategic entrepreneur capable of building a resilient enterprise.

It's surprisingly easy to mistake economic activity for entrepreneurship. You bake cakes at home and sell them to neighbors? You're making money, yes but does that alone mean you're running a business? You import T-shirts from a wholesale site and resell them on Instagram? It's commerce, but is it a structured enterprise? This misunderstanding is so prevalent that many small-scale entrepreneurs find themselves years into their ventures without ever actually building a business. What they have instead is a job they've created for themselves, often one with less stability and more stress than a conventional employment role. The work is real, the money is real, but the foundation is often shaky because the focus has been on immediate transactions, not long-term systems. This "transaction trap" locks people into a reactive mode, constantly chasing sales, firefighting operational issues, and relying heavily on their own time and presence to keep things running. The moment the founder stops working, the income dries up not because the market no longer exists, but because the business was never designed to function independently.

Real businesses, even small ones are defined by structure. This includes clear workflows, repeatable processes, consistent branding, financial tracking, and defined roles, even if it's just one person wearing multiple hats. Take, for example, a street food vendor versus a small local restaurant. The vendor may be excellent at cooking and attract a loyal clientele. But if that person were to fall ill or take a vacation, the entire operation could halt. There may be no recipes written down, no inventory system, and no backup cook. Contrast that with the restaurant, where menus are standardized, staff are trained, suppliers are on schedule, and the owner doesn't need to be present daily for things to operate. That's structure. Structure turns business activity into a system. And systems are what allow entrepreneurs to eventually step back and let the business function and grow without their constant involvement. Whether you're selling handmade crafts or offering local repair services, the question to ask is: "Can this run without me? Or have I simply built a cage for myself that I happen to own?"

At the center of every real business is the creation and delivery of value. This concept is often confused with volume which is the number of units sold, the footfall in a shop, the clicks on an ad. But value is deeper. It's about how well your product or service solves a real problem, fulfills a need, or improves someone's life.

Small-scale businesses sometimes overlook this in favor of quick wins. Drop-shipping trending products or mimicking what's currently popular can bring fast revenue, but it often lacks staying power because it's not rooted in authentic value creation. True business thinking starts with the customer: Who are they? What do they need? How are they currently solving their problems? How can I do it better? Value also influences pricing power and customer loyalty. A customer who sees real value in what you offer is less likely to haggle and more likely to return. They become part of a community, not just a transaction. And this, in turn, fuels one of the most powerful assets in small business: word-of-mouth.

Business is not a moment; it's a continuum. It evolves, adapts, and grows but only when approached strategically. Strategy involves making intentional choices about how you do business. It includes market positioning, branding, customer experience, competitive analysis, and growth planning. Even a small side hustle can benefit from strategy. Consider a freelance graphic designer. Without strategy, they may take whatever jobs come their way, charge inconsistent rates, and constantly chase new clients. But with a strategy, they may focus on a niche (e.g., branding for wellness businesses), create a signature service package, develop referral systems, and eventually build a small agency. The work may look similar on the surface, but the structure and intent behind it are vastly different. Crucially, systems and strategy together allow for scalability. Scalability doesn't always mean opening 100 franchises. It could mean adding more customers without adding equal stress. It might mean productizing a service (e.g., turning a consulting process into a course) or using technology to reduce manual work. When systems support your daily operations and strategy drives your long-term direction, you're no longer just doing business. You are building one.

Many small businesses start from a place of passion. Someone loves cooking, designing, teaching, or fixing things and they decide to monetize it. Passion is a powerful starting point, but it's not enough. Without intention, passion can become chaotic. The work is enjoyable, but the income is erratic. The owner is busy, but the business isn't progressing.

Intentionality means treating the venture like a business from day one, even if it's small. This includes setting goals, tracking finances, documenting processes, analyzing performance, and planning ahead. It means thinking like an owner, not just a worker. You begin to see your offering as a solution, your customer as a relationship, and your time as an investment. This mental shift is what professionalizes a business. It transforms a "side hustle" into an enterprise, a passion into a platform. And it's accessible to anyone willing to adopt a builder's mindset, one that prioritizes systems, value, and strategic growth.

Perhaps the most defining characteristic of a true business is the intention to build something that lasts. This could mean different things for different entrepreneurs. For some, it's a multi-generational family operation. For others, it's a well-run venture that allows personal freedom and community impact. Longevity requires resilience both operational and emotional. Businesses that last aren't the ones with the flashiest marketing or the highest early profits. They are the ones that understand their ecosystem, know their customers deeply, maintain lean but effective operations, and adapt without losing their core identity. This mindset also includes preparation for succession, potential sale, or transition. Even if you don't plan to sell your business, building it as if you could forces you to create something independent of yourself, something with clear value in the market and structured systems under the hood.

To define a business only by the act of buying and selling is to ignore its most powerful aspects. For small-scale entrepreneurs, the goal isn't to imitate large corporations, but to internalize the principles that make them successful: clarity of purpose, operational discipline, customer-centricity, and adaptability. When these are present even in a modest enterprise the result is no longer just a hustle. It is a business in the truest sense. So, as you embark on or refine your journey, ask yourself: Am I simply making money? Or am I building something that can grow, serve, and sustain? The difference between the two is not just academic; it's the foundation on which everything else is built.

In today's economy, where monetizing skills and interests is easier than ever, it's common to see people earning money from baking cakes, designing graphics, selling vintage clothes, or tutoring online. But does making money automatically mean you're running a business? The answer is more nuanced and much more important than many realize. A critical step in the journey of any small-scale entrepreneur is the honest assessment of what they've built. Is it a hobby, a hustle, or a business? Understanding the differences isn't just about labels but it's about clarity, direction, and sustainability.

A hobby is something you do primarily for personal satisfaction. You might knit, paint, bake, write, or build model airplanes. It may even generate occasional income, but that's incidental and not intentional. The hobby exists whether or not anyone is watching, paying, or benefiting. You do it because you love it. Key traits of a hubby include passion-driven, not profit-driven, sporadic time investment, Inconsistent or no income, no formal structure (e.g., no branding, pricing model, or customer base) and success is measured in personal enjoyment, not revenue or impact. Hobbies are essential for well-being and creativity, and they often serve as the seed of future businesses. But the problem arises when people mistake their hobby for a business or try to force it into becoming one without proper planning. For example, someone who loves making candles may start giving them to friends or selling a few at craft fairs. They might call it a business, but if there are no systems in place such as no costing, no sales strategy, no consistency as they're likely still operating at a hobby level.

A hustle, or "side hustle" as it's often called, is a step beyond the hobby. Here, the primary goal *is* to earn money but usually without long-term vision, consistent processes, or formal structure. Hustles often emerge from necessity or opportunity. Someone needs extra cash, notices a market gap, or has a monetizable skill so they start selling something or offering a service. Hustling is entrepreneurial in spirit but rarely strategic in execution.

They are revenue-driven, but often short-term focused, operated solo with minimal investment, heavily reliant on the owner's time and effort, inconsistent branding, pricing, and customer retention and lacks formal systems like bookkeeping, marketing plans, or scalable operations. The hustle mindset is powerful as it's resourceful, adaptable, and bold. Many great businesses started as hustles. But where it falls short is in scalability and sustainability. When everything revolves around the founder including their time, energy, and decisions, the venture quickly hits a ceiling. Many side hustlers eventually burn out or plateau because they don't shift their mindset or invest in building infrastructure. They stay stuck in a cycle of survival rather than growth.

A business is fundamentally different. It still may be small, solo-run, or home-based but it operates with intentionality, repeatability, and growth in mind. A business is not just a way to earn; it's a system designed to deliver value, serve a market, and produce consistent income whether the founder is present or not. It has clear purpose and target market, defined brand, product, and customer experience, strategic pricing and marketing models, operational systems (e.g., order processing, customer service, inventory) and long-term planning (e.g., growth, scaling, team building). Business owners look at metrics, test strategies, invest in tools, and build partnerships. They plan for taxes, register their businesses, and think in terms of quarters and years, not just weeks or gigs. Most importantly, they build systems that allow for predictability and growth. Where hobbies and hustles are reactive, businesses are proactive. They move from just doing the work to building a machine that does the work.

Some might ask does it really matter what I call it? If I enjoy what I'm doing and I'm making money, who cares if it's a hustle or a business? It matters because each path has different requirements, risks, and potential. Mislabeling what you do can lead to confusion, burnout, or missed opportunity. If you're running a hustle but calling it a business, you might skip essential steps like registering legally, paying taxes, or reinvesting in infrastructure. If you're calling your hobby a business, you might become discouraged when it doesn't make money or scale like others.

A business demands more of you but it also promises more in return. By understanding where you are and where you want to go, you can match your effort to your ambition. If you want freedom, growth, and impact, you must be willing to build systems, develop strategies, and think long-term. A hobby might cost you money. A hustle might earn you quick cash but no long-term wealth. A business when built properly becomes an asset. It can generate recurring income, employ others, or even be sold.

Many small-scale entrepreneurs operate in the gray area between hustle and business and that's okay. The important thing is to recognize when it's time to level up. Here are some signals. You're consistently making income but feel overwhelmed or disorganized.

You want to grow but don't know how. You're tired of chasing clients or orders manually. You see competitors with systems and wonder how they manage. You crave more stability, freedom, or impact from your work. If this sounds like you, then it's time to start thinking and acting like a business.

The transition from hobby or hustle to business doesn't happen overnight. It's a journey of gradual changes, each reinforcing the other. Here are some initial steps. Stop selling "everything to everyone." Focus on what you do best, who it helps, and how it's different from others. Clarity in your offer attracts better customers and simplifies your operations. Track revenue, expenses, and profits. Understand your pricing. Many hustlers undercharge because they don't calculate their real costs or value. Financial literacy is non-negotiable in business. Document how you do things such as how you take orders, deliver products, follow up with clients. Even simple tools like spreadsheets or templates can reduce chaos and prepare you for growth. A professional brand builds trust. You don't need expensive logos or a website at first, but consistency in how you present yourself goes a long way. Think beyond next week. What does success look like in a year? Three years? Do you want to hire help, launch new products, or open a shop? Set goals and work backwards from them.

Perhaps the hardest part of this evolution is not logistical but emotional. Many people cling to their hobby or hustle identity because it feels safe. There's less pressure, less formality, fewer expectations. But it also limits your potential. Transitioning into a business owner means embracing responsibility, strategy, and leadership. It means shifting from "I like doing this" to "I'm building something bigger than myself." That can be intimidating but it's also incredibly empowering. When you stop seeing your venture as just a gig and start treating it as an entity that deserves structure, systems, and respect, everything changes. You start making decisions differently. You attract different clients. You reclaim your time. You step into a new identity, one of an entrepreneur, not just an earner.

Not everyone wants to run a business and that's perfectly fine. Some people find joy and fulfillment in keeping things at a hobby or hustle level. The key is intentionality. If your goal is freedom, scalability, or legacy, then you'll need to move beyond hustling and build the foundations of a real business. But if your priority is expression, flexibility, or supplemental income, a hobby or side gig may be enough. There's no wrong answer, only an honest one.

Many people who engage in commerce think they are running a business simply because money changes hands. They sell food, fix electronics, resell items online, or offer freelance services and feel justified in calling themselves business owners. But earning income from an activity does not automatically make that activity a business. What differentiates a genuine enterprise from a hustle is not how much money is made or how busy the founder is, but how the entire operation is structured from how it's built, managed, and positioned for repeatable success.

A real business has core components that function together to create consistency, value, and potential for growth. Without these components, what someone is running might still generate revenue, but it will always rely on personal hustle, spontaneity, and luck. It becomes a cycle of effort-for-money, with no infrastructure to support sustainability or scale. So, what makes a business whole?

What are the unseen pillars that separate a sustainable enterprise from an improvised operation? To answer that, we must look beneath the surface.

First, there must be a clearly defined product or service. This might seem obvious, but in reality, many small-scale entrepreneurs operate without precision. They offer a broad range of things, switching frequently based on trends, customer requests, or personal whim. But real businesses offer something specific, well-developed, and replicable. The offering is not just a product; it's a solution. It addresses a need, fills a gap, or solves a problem and it does so in a way that can be consistently delivered without reinventing the wheel each time. This level of clarity creates the foundation for everything else, from branding to customer service.

Once the offering is defined, the business must have a target market. Too many early entrepreneurs make the mistake of trying to serve everyone, assuming that a wider net will bring in more customers. But in truth, successful businesses are built on specificity. They know who they're for. They understand their ideal customers intimately such as their needs, preferences, behaviors, and pain points. This depth of knowledge allows the business to tailor not just its products, but its messaging, pricing, and delivery in a way that resonates deeply. A real business doesn't wait for customers to come; it knows exactly whom it's trying to reach and goes after them with intention.

With a clear offer and a clear audience, the next core component is the revenue model. This is more than just charging a price. It's about understanding how money flows through the business, how it is generated, when it comes in, what costs are associated with earning it, and how profits are realized. Too often, people price based on gut feeling or competitor imitation without understanding their own cost structures or value proposition. But a real business knows its numbers. It understands margins, break-even points, and profitability. It plans around cash flow, not just sales. Without this awareness, growth becomes a risk rather than an opportunity, because each new customer or sale could strain an already fragile system.

Supporting all of this is the operational framework such as the internal systems that keep things running smoothly behind the scenes. This includes supply chains, inventory management, order processing, delivery logistics, customer service protocols, and quality control. Operations are what transform vision into execution. Without strong operations, even the best product and best marketing can fall apart, because the business can't deliver consistently or professionally. Many small business owners fall into the trap of doing everything manually, from taking orders via WhatsApp to remembering each customer's preferences by memory. That might work at the very beginning, but over time, these fragile systems lead to burnout, errors, and lost opportunities. A real business builds systems even simple ones to ensure consistency, reduce stress, and make scaling possible.

Another core component is branding, which is often misunderstood. Branding is not just a logo or a catchy name; it is the entire experience a customer has with the business. It's how people feel when they hear the business name, how they perceive its values, how much they trust its promises. In a world where choices are endless, branding is what creates differentiation. Two shops may sell the same handmade soap, but the one with a clear, compelling, and consistent brand will win customer loyalty, even at a higher price. That's because real businesses invest in perception, not just product. They create stories, values, and identities that resonate beyond the transaction.

Perhaps the most overlooked yet vital component is the ability to scale. A business that cannot grow is one that is ultimately limited by its founder's time, energy, or physical reach. Scaling does not mean turning a neighborhood kiosk into a national chain rather it means building a structure that can handle more customers, orders, or impact without collapsing. This often requires automation, delegation, digital tools, or physical infrastructure, depending on the industry. But more than that, it requires mindset. The business must be built to grow from day one even if growth is not immediate. The processes, the team culture, the financial planning, all must be oriented around sustainability and expansion, not just survival.

At the heart of all these components lies a philosophy of intentionality. Real businesses are not reactive; they are designed. Every aspect is deliberate. The founder doesn't just ask, "How do I make money today?" but "How does this decision contribute to the long-term success and stability of my business?" That shift in thinking is what elevates a side hustle into a sustainable enterprise. It's not about perfection or size. Many powerful businesses are run by one or two people out of a single room but what makes them real is the presence of structure, clarity, and strategy.

It's also important to understand that these components do not exist in isolation. They interact constantly. The clarity of the offer informs the marketing strategy. The understanding of the target market affects how operations are structured. The revenue model influences product development. Each decision has ripple effects, which is why piecemeal improvement rarely works. A business must be built holistically, with each element reinforcing the others.

This is where many entrepreneurs get stuck. They optimize one area while ignoring others. They pour money into marketing without refining the product, or they obsess over packaging without understanding their pricing. But a real business requires balance. Each component must grow in sync. That's the difference between building a brand that lasts and spinning your wheels in a never-ending loop of effort. To move from hustle to enterprise, one must begin to see the business as an ecosystem which is living, breathing, and evolving. Like any ecosystem, it needs balance, resilience, and adaptability. You don't need to get it perfect from the start, but you must be committed to building and refining these components over time. That is what makes a business strong. That is what makes it real.

The moment you start thinking in systems, identifying repeatable processes, and designing your operations to support not just today's sales but tomorrow's possibilities, you are no longer just doing business. You are building one. You've moved beyond the informal stage. You've crossed into the realm where your venture can grow, provide, employ, and endure.

Ultimately, the core components of a real business are not mysterious or unattainable. They are accessible to anyone willing to step out of the daily grind and look at their work with fresh eyes. The entrepreneur who stops long enough to ask, "How can this run better without me?" is already on the right path. Because that question, simple, yet powerful is the beginning of every great business story.

If there's one defining factor that separates enduring businesses from fleeting ventures, it's not a clever product, a lucky market, or even deep funding. It's the mindset of the person behind it. While structure, systems, and strategy are all critical, they stem from something deeper, the way an entrepreneur thinks. Building a real business begins with a mental shift, a conscious transition from executing tasks to cultivating a vision, from reacting to leading, from surviving to creating.

Most people who start small businesses begin as doers. They bake the cakes, fix the appliances, design the websites, or cut the hair. Their skills become their livelihood, and their income depends directly on how much they produce. This is where nearly everyone begins, by trading time and effort for money. But for a business to grow beyond that point, the person at the center must shift their identity. They must stop seeing themselves solely as a worker and start seeing themselves as a builder, a strategist, a leader. This change doesn't happen naturally. It requires a deliberate rethinking of one's role, priorities, and relationship to work.

The mindset of a worker is often rooted in the present moment. It focuses on immediate outcomes such as fulfilling an order, pleasing a client, closing a sale. But the entrepreneurial mindset lives in the future. It asks: What am I building? What does this look like in one year, three years, five years? It's not about abandoning the day-to-day, but about seeing the daily actions as bricks in a much larger structure. This long-term vision allows entrepreneurs to make decisions that may not pay off immediately, but that position the business for resilience and scale over time.

Thinking like an entrepreneur means learning to detach from the idea that your value is based solely on how hard you work. It means recognizing that growth often requires doing less of the labor yourself so you can spend more time building systems, developing people, refining offers, and making strategic decisions. In a small business, especially in the early days, this can feel counterintuitive. It can feel irresponsible even. Why spend hours documenting a process when you could just get the job done? Why hire someone at a cost when you could do it yourself for free? But these are precisely the kinds of questions that separate a business operator from a business owner. At its core, the entrepreneurial mindset is about leverage. It's about identifying how to create the most value with the least amount of personal effort not because you're lazy, but because you understand that time is your most limited and precious resource. Entrepreneurs learn to think in terms of outcomes, not hours. They ask, "How can this process be done faster, better, or by someone else?" They begin to measure success not by how busy they are, but by how efficiently the business can run and grow, even in their absence.

But adopting this mindset is often a struggle because it challenges so many deeply held beliefs, especially among small-scale entrepreneurs who built their identities around working hard. Many were raised to believe that effort equals worth, that sweat and sacrifice are the markers of success. And while hard work certainly plays a role, it is not a business model. The problem with relying solely on effort is that it has a ceiling. You only have so many hours, so much energy, so much personal capacity. Businesses that depend entirely on their owner's output can never outgrow that owner's limitations.

This is why mindset is the first domino. Before you hire a team, invest in software, or scale your marketing, you must believe and truly believe that your business is capable of existing as something larger than you. You must be willing to let go of control, embrace risk, and prioritize vision over comfort. You must be willing to disappoint a few clients in the short term by restructuring how you serve them, if it means building a more sustainable operation in the long term. You must be willing to invest today in tools, training, or talent that may not pay off until tomorrow. These decisions are not made by people stuck in the hustle mindset. They are made by people who are building something that can stand on its own.

Thinking like an entrepreneur also means learning how to interpret failure differently. When workers make mistakes, the consequences are often personal such as a bad review, a missed sale, a stressful day. But entrepreneurs view failures as data. They extract lessons, adapt quickly, and try again. They understand that failure is part of iteration, not a sign to stop. This resilience, not just the ability to endure, but the ability to evolve is at the heart of entrepreneurial thinking.

Equally important is the shift from scarcity to abundance. Many small business owners operate with a scarcity mindset, fearing competition, hoarding control, underpricing their services, or avoiding collaboration. But entrepreneurs with a true ownership mentality see opportunity everywhere. They understand that partnerships can multiply reach, that competitors can validate markets, and that pricing should reflect value, not insecurity. They recognize that money is a tool, not a trophy and that investing in growth is not an expense but a necessity.

This abundance mindset also extends to how entrepreneurs view their role in the world. They start to see their business not just as a means of survival, but as a vehicle for impact. They realize that their choices in sourcing, hiring, pricing, messaging shape the world around them. They begin to build businesses with values, not just goals. They ask how they can improve lives, solve real problems, create meaningful jobs, or inspire others. This sense of purpose becomes a powerful driver, anchoring the business in something deeper than profit.

Another key aspect of this mindset shift is time orientation. Workers live task to task. Hustlers live day to day. Entrepreneurs live in quarters and years. They structure their work in cycles. They set strategic goals. They evaluate performance over time, not just in isolated moments. This ability to zoom out and see the bigger picture gives them clarity when things get messy and focus when things get noisy. It allows them to say no to distractions and stay committed to their direction.

Yet perhaps the most radical shift of all is the decision to think beyond you. True entrepreneurs understand that their business is not just about them. It's about the customers they serve, the team they may lead, the legacy they may leave. This shift is humbling. It forces you to confront your limitations and embrace your potential. It invites you to stop being the hero of your story and start being the architect of a system that can empower others.

None of this is easy. In fact, it's one of the hardest parts of entrepreneurship. Building a website or designing a product is relatively straightforward compared to shifting the way you think, make decisions, and define success. But it is also the most rewarding transformation. Because once your mind shifts, your entire business shifts with it. You start attracting better clients, making sharper choices, and creating something that truly works, not just for you, but for the people it touches. You begin to delegate, not because you're overwhelmed, but because you're strategic. You begin to market with clarity, not desperation. You begin to price with confidence, not apology. And you begin to lead, not just labor.

In the end, thinking like an entrepreneur means seeing your business not as a job you've created for yourself, but as a living, breathing entity that needs nurturing, direction, and structure. It means seeing yourself not as the engine, but as the engineer, the one who designs how it all works together. It means releasing the need to do everything and embracing the responsibility to build something bigger than your effort alone.

Every great business begins long before the first sale is made. It begins with an idea of not just of what to offer, but why it matters, who it serves, and where it's headed. In the rush to earn, many small business owners skip this step. They dive into doing before ever defining their direction. But in time, the lack of clarity catches up with them. Sales plateau, motivation fades, and decisions become reactive instead of strategic. That's because no matter how hardworking or talented you are, a business without a vision is a business without a compass.

Vision is not just a statement on a wall or a fancy paragraph on a website. It is the deep, internal understanding of what you're building and why it matters. It is the picture in your mind of what success looks like not just in financial terms, but in terms of impact, legacy, and contribution. Your vision shapes the size and scope of your ambitions. It determines whether you're building a small neighborhood shop, a regional service provider, or a brand that touches lives across borders. More importantly, vision keeps you going when the path is unclear. It becomes the emotional fuel when circumstances challenge your resolve.

Alongside vision stands mission which is the actionable expression of purpose. If vision is the destination, mission is the map. It defines what you do, for whom, and how. It turns inspiration into intention. A clear mission helps customers understand your role in their lives. It helps employees understand their role in your company. It turns your business from a money-making engine into a purpose-driven endeavor. Without a mission, a business risks drifting toward what's profitable instead of what's meaningful. But with a mission, every choice can be measured against a deeper standard.

Far too often, small-scale entrepreneurs see vision and mission as luxuries and nice ideas for larger companies, but not necessary for people still figuring things out. But in truth, these principles are most powerful at the small scale. That's because at this stage, your business is still flexible, still malleable. You have the chance to shape it intentionally before the demands of growth begin to shape it for you. Without vision, you'll end up chasing trends, copying competitors, or simply responding to whoever pays. With vision, you lead. You build with direction. You turn down what doesn't align, and you double down on what does.

Vision also defines growth or more precisely, the kind of growth that matters to you. Not every business needs to scale exponentially. Not every entrepreneur wants to build an empire. For some, success means freedom and flexibility. For others, it means community impact or creative fulfillment. There is no one-size-fits-all trajectory. But what matters is that you grow intentionally, with clarity on where you want to go and what you're willing to trade to get there. Growth without direction is just expansion. But growth with intention becomes evolution.

Intentional growth means setting milestones that align with your values. It means asking not just "How much do I want to earn?" but "What kind of life do I want to live?" "What kind of team do I want to build?" "What kind of legacy do I want to leave?" These questions do not have immediate answers. They evolve as you evolve. But asking them early and often keeps your business grounded in purpose. It ensures that every step forward is a step toward something, not just away from where you began. This kind of clarity also simplifies decision-making. When you know your vision and mission, you no longer need to chase every opportunity. You no longer fear saying no. You begin to attract the right customers, the right collaborators, the right investors and people who resonate with your story because it's consistent, coherent, and clear. In this way, intentional growth is not just a strategy; it's a magnet. It draws in alignment. And alignment is where real momentum lives.

To grow intentionally also means embracing the idea that you are not just building a business but you are building your business. That distinction matters. Anyone can run a generic operation. But when your business is rooted in your values, driven by your vision, and expressed through your mission, it becomes a unique reflection of who you are and what you stand for. It becomes a space where your principles are practiced, where your skills are honored, and where your dreams are translated into systems, products, and relationships. That is when business stops being just work and starts becoming a way of life.

Still, this kind of growth does not happen by accident. It requires periodic reflection. It demands that you step out of the day-to-day to assess your progress, realign your goals, and reimagine your future. Many entrepreneurs get caught in the rhythm of routine such as servicing clients, managing inventory, answering messages without ever stepping back to ask, "Is this still what I want?" Intentional growth requires that pause. It requires discipline to ask difficult questions and courage to make uncomfortable changes.

Sometimes, the most intentional decision you can make is to pivot. Maybe the market changed. Maybe your life did. Maybe the work that once thrilled you now drains you. That's not failure but that's awareness. Businesses are not meant to be static. They are living systems. Vision and mission are not contracts; they are compasses. As long as you stay connected to what matters, change can be a sign of maturity, not confusion.

Intentional growth also respects pace. Not every business is meant to scale fast. The culture of "10x everything" has pushed many small business owners into unhealthy cycles of comparison and overextension. But sustainable growth is not about speed and about strength. It's about building at the pace your systems can support, your market can handle, and your life can sustain. Some of the strongest businesses in the world grew slowly not because they lacked ambition, but because they respected the process.

Part of that process is reinvestment of not just of money, but of energy, creativity, and attention. As your business grows, your role changes. You move from doing the work to directing the work. From selling products to shaping strategy. From being the brand to building one. And that shift, too, must be intentional. It's not about doing less, but doing differently. It's about letting go of things that no longer serve your highest impact and leaning into the work that moves the vision forward. The final piece of intentional growth is storytelling. Your vision and mission are not just internal guides, they are external messages. The more clearly you articulate them, the more powerful your brand becomes. People want to support businesses they believe in. They want to buy from founders with conviction, not just convenience. They want to connect with the *why*, not just the *what*. Your story is your strongest currency. When told with clarity and confidence, it turns customers into advocates, clients into collaborators, and employees into believers.

And this brings us full circle. The decision to grow intentionally is a decision to lead not just your business, but your life. It is a refusal to drift. A refusal to build blindly. A refusal to settle for busy when you could be building something meaningful. That's what vision does. It reminds you of the bigger picture. That's what mission does. It gives you a daily reason to keep showing up. And that's what intentional growth does. It turns your business into a journey and one that evolves with you, challenges you, and ultimately, transforms you. Because in the end, you are not just growing a business, you are growing into the person who can lead it. The systems, the strategies, the products, they all matter but they mean nothing without direction, without purpose and without clarity. So if you take nothing else from this chapter, take this: the most important thing you can do for your business is to know what it stands for, who it serves, and where it's going. Everything else, every decision, every investment, every late night and early morning should flow from that.

Your vision is your North Star. Your mission is your compass. Your growth is the path you walk. Walk it with intention, and you won't just run a business, you'll build one that matters.

CHAPTER TWO
LAYING THE GROUNDWORK

Building a successful small-scale business begins with one of the most fundamental yet often overlooked elements: the business model. While many entrepreneurs focus their energy on products, marketing, or sales, the business model is the invisible architecture that determines whether all those efforts translate into sustained value creation and growth. It is the framework that explains how your business creates, delivers, and captures value is the blueprint for turning ideas and labor into revenue and impact. Understanding and intentionally crafting a business model is not just a strategic exercise; it is the cornerstone upon which every decision and action rests.

A business model answers the question: How does this business make money? But this question, deceptively simple, opens into a far more complex landscape. The answer is not just about pricing or products, but about the relationships between your customers, your value proposition, your resources, your channels, and your revenue streams. It's about designing an interconnected system where every part supports the other, creating a sustainable flow of value from you to your customers and back again. Without this clarity, a business risks floundering and trying tactics that don't fit, investing in ideas that don't pay off, or worse, burning out its owner without building lasting momentum.

For many small business owners, the business model evolves unconsciously. They start with a skill or a passion such as making crafts, offering consulting, providing landscaping and begin exchanging those services for money. Early success often comes from direct trade: hours worked for dollars earned. This is the familiar model of the solo operator, and it works well enough at first. But as soon as the business owner seeks to grow beyond their personal capacity, cracks begin to show. The model that depends entirely on personal time and effort creates a ceiling, limiting growth and threatening sustainability.

Crafting a business model that works means stepping back to see the bigger picture. It requires a shift from thinking in tasks to thinking in systems. Instead of asking "What will I sell?" the entrepreneur must ask, "Who am I serving, and how will I consistently deliver value to them in a way that supports my goals?" This shift in perspective lays the groundwork for intentional design. Every element of the business from product development, marketing channels, pricing strategies, customer relationships can be aligned and optimized only after the business model is understood and articulated.

One of the most useful ways to approach this process is to think in terms of the classic components of a business model: value proposition, customer segments, channels, customer relationships, revenue streams, key resources, key activities, key partnerships, and cost structure. While these terms may sound technical, they describe the simple reality of any business. For example, the value proposition is the promise you make to your customers such as what problem you solve or what desire you fulfill. Customer segments define who you serve, recognizing that different groups may require different approaches. Channels are the ways you reach and deliver value to customers, whether through a storefront, online platforms, or direct sales. Customer relationships describe how you interact with and retain those customers. Revenue streams show how the money flows in. Key resources and activities outline what you need to operate effectively. Partnerships help fill gaps and create leverage. Costs reveal the expenses that must be managed carefully to maintain profitability.

Even as you learn these components, it is critical to understand that no business model is perfect from the start. Crafting a model is an iterative process. It involves testing assumptions, gathering feedback, and adapting as you learn what works and what doesn't. This mindset of experimentation is crucial because markets change, customers evolve, and competition shifts constantly. A static model becomes brittle; a flexible one endures. This is why some of the most successful entrepreneurs embrace the business model canvas or similar tools or visual frameworks that help map out and adjust these interconnected elements in a dynamic way.

Consider a small bakery as an example. The owner's value proposition might be freshly baked, artisanal bread made from organic ingredients. Their customer segments could include health-conscious locals, nearby cafes buying wholesale, and event planners ordering specialty cakes. Channels might include a physical storefront, online ordering, and local farmers' markets. Customer relationships could range from friendly in-person service to subscription bread delivery. Revenue streams might come from direct sales, wholesale contracts, and seasonal promotions. Key resources include skilled bakers, quality ingredients, ovens, and a delivery vehicle. Key activities revolve around baking, marketing, and customer service. Partnerships might include local farms supplying ingredients or delivery services. Costs include rent, wages, utilities, and marketing. By mapping this out, the bakery owner can see where value is created and where bottlenecks or risks lie. For example, if most revenue depends on wholesale contracts, what happens if one client leaves? Should they diversify? If in-person sales slow, can online orders compensate? This clarity enables better decisions about where to invest time and money, and where to innovate.

It's important to remember that a business model is not merely a financial plan. It is a strategic narrative that aligns every part of the business to deliver value consistently and sustainably. It shapes how you think about your customers, how you design your offerings, and how you measure success. Without a clear model, you may be selling products or services, but you are not truly building a business.

Crafting a business model also helps you set realistic expectations and goals. When you know how your business makes money, you can forecast revenues and expenses more accurately, identify break-even points, and plan for investment or cash flow needs. It reduces uncertainty and guides your growth strategy. More than that, it gives you a language to communicate your business to partners, investors, and team members which are essential when you begin to delegate or seek support.

Many small-scale entrepreneurs struggle with this because the business model concept feels abstract or overwhelming. They worry about "doing it wrong" or feel stuck in day-to-day operations. The key is to start small and build gradually. Begin by writing down your current assumptions: Who are your customers? What are you offering? How do you get paid? Then test these assumptions through conversations, sales data, and customer feedback. Refine your understanding regularly. One powerful insight is that your business model can and should evolve as you grow. What worked when you were selling one-on-one may not work when you scale to a team or broader market. For instance, a freelance graphic designer might begin with hourly billing but later develop packages or subscription services to create predictable income. A home-based crafts business might start by selling at local fairs but transition to e-commerce and wholesale accounts. Recognizing that your business model is a living framework keeps you adaptable and resilient.

Crafting a business model that works means embracing the mindset that your business is more than your current activities. It is a system designed to deliver ongoing value. When you see your business this way, you start to prioritize investments in systems, partnerships, and processes that create leverage. You focus not just on working harder, but on working smarter. You understand that every element of your business must fit together cohesively to support growth and sustainability.

This clarity is what separates hobbyists and side hustles from true businesses. The hobbyist may create value for a few customers but lacks the systematization and scalability that a business model provides. The side hustler juggles projects and income sources but may not have clarity on how to build lasting momentum. The entrepreneur who crafts and evolves a coherent business model builds a foundation capable of withstanding challenges, adapting to change, and thriving in complexity.

In this sense, your business model is not just a plan but it's your guiding framework, your lens for decision-making, and your pathway to intentional growth. It frees you from the chaos of reactive decisions and empowers you to lead with purpose. It turns a collection of activities into a cohesive enterprise. So, as you lay the groundwork for your small business, commit time and energy to crafting a business model that truly works for you. Use it as a living document, revisiting and refining it as you learn. Build your business not just on passion or product, but on a clear understanding of how value flows from you, through your systems, to your customers, and back. That is the secret to turning a small business into a lasting enterprise.

In the journey of building a small-scale business, vision gives you the "why" and the business model gives you the "how." Yet, without clearly defined goals, you risk wandering aimlessly. Goals act as the roadmap, transforming broad ambitions into actionable milestones. They serve as checkpoints, guiding decisions, motivating action, and providing tangible markers of progress. Without them, even the most promising business risks stagnation or burnout, as effort becomes scattered and momentum slips away.

Setting defined goals is often seen as a corporate or large-business practice, something unnecessary or overly formal for smaller enterprises. However, the opposite is true. Small businesses benefit immensely from clear goals because they provide focus and alignment in the face of daily distractions and challenges. When every task is weighed against a clear objective, it becomes easier to prioritize and say no to what doesn't serve your growth. Goals become the compass that keeps the business on track amid uncertainty.

Effective goals are not vague or aspirational statements. "I want to grow my business" or "I want to be successful" are well-meaning, but they lack the clarity needed to spark action. Defined goals are specific, measurable, achievable, relevant, and time-bound, in other words, SMART. This framework transforms nebulous desires into concrete targets. For example, instead of "grow sales," a defined goal might be "increase monthly revenue by 15% over the next six months." Such specificity allows you to plan strategies, allocate resources, and evaluate success with precision.

The process of setting goals forces a business owner to consider both the short and long term. Short-term goals might focus on immediate needs: launching a new product, acquiring initial customers, or optimizing operations. Long-term goals set the vision for where the business wants to be in a year, five years, or beyond. These layered goals create a dynamic roadmap, breaking down the big picture into manageable steps. This reduces overwhelm, making growth feel attainable rather than daunting.

Goals also function as motivational anchors. Entrepreneurship, especially at the small scale, is a marathon, not a sprint. The road is littered with setbacks, unexpected costs, and moments of doubt. Well-defined goals provide milestones to celebrate, fueling confidence and reinforcing progress. They create a rhythm to the work, marking a series of small victories rather than an endless grind. This positive reinforcement is crucial for maintaining momentum and resilience. Furthermore, defined goals foster accountability. When goals are documented and revisited regularly, they move from abstract hopes to commitments. They invite reflection: What's working? What isn't? What adjustments are needed? This continuous feedback loop is the lifeblood of agile business management. Without goals, it's easy to coast or lose direction; with them, you create a discipline of constant learning and improvement.

Goal-setting also helps in resource management. Time, money, and energy are finite, especially in small businesses where owners wear many hats. Clear goals inform decisions about where to invest these resources. Should you spend money on advertising or product development? Should you hire help or refine your existing processes? By aligning every decision with specific goals, you ensure resources are used efficiently, maximizing impact.

Importantly, goals should not be set in isolation. They thrive when connected to the broader vision and mission of the business. A goal to increase social media followers makes little sense if your business's mission centers on personalized, face-to-face service. Conversely, goals aligned with your core purpose help maintain authenticity and strengthen your brand identity. This alignment ensures that growth does not come at the cost of your business's soul.

Many entrepreneurs hesitate to set ambitious goals, fearing failure or overcommitment. But setting goals is not about rigid targets that must be met at all costs; it's about intentional direction. Goals can be adjusted as you learn and grow. They are tools for clarity, not chains of pressure. In fact, flexible goal-setting involves revisiting and refining goals regularly is a hallmark of adaptive, resilient businesses. The practice of goal-setting also fosters strategic thinking. When you map out what you want to achieve, you naturally begin to ask how. What marketing strategies will move the needle? What partnerships will accelerate growth? What systems will improve efficiency? This forward-thinking approach shifts the business from reactive to proactive. It builds confidence in leadership and prepares the ground for intentional growth.

Equally, goals serve as communication tools. Whether you're collaborating with employees, partners, or investors, clearly defined goals provide a shared understanding of what success looks like. This alignment strengthens teamwork and helps everyone pull in the same direction. In the absence of clear goals, efforts become fragmented, and motivation wanes. Setting goals also invites reflection on values and priorities. Not all growth is desirable. Some businesses may prioritize profitability, others sustainability, and others community impact. Goals help articulate these priorities in actionable terms. They encourage you to think critically about trade-offs, such as balancing quality versus quantity, or growth versus work-life balance. This self-awareness is vital for building a business that serves not just your customers, but your life.

Finally, defined goals build confidence through clarity. When you know what you want and can track your progress, you gain a sense of control in the often unpredictable world of small business. This clarity reduces anxiety and opens space for creativity and innovation. It empowers you to make decisions grounded in purpose rather than panic. In sum, setting defined goals is not a bureaucratic exercise reserved for large corporations. It is a powerful act of leadership and self-care for small business owners. It turns abstract dreams into concrete steps, aligns daily efforts with long-term vision, and builds momentum through measurable progress. When crafted thoughtfully and revisited regularly, goals become the roadmap to success, guiding your business from where it is today to where you want it to be tomorrow.

When starting a small-scale business, one of the most crucial decisions you will face early on is choosing the legal structure under which your enterprise will operate. This choice carries far-reaching implications such as influencing everything from your tax obligations and personal liability to your ability to raise capital and grow. While it might seem like a technical or bureaucratic hurdle, selecting the right legal structure is foundational to shaping how your business functions, protects you as the owner, and interacts with customers, partners, and regulatory bodies. Understanding this choice deeply and intentionally is an essential part of laying the groundwork for a sustainable and scalable business.

A legal structure defines the legal identity of your business. It determines whether the business is considered an extension of you personally or a separate entity altogether. This distinction matters because it affects your personal risk exposure. If your business operates as a sole proprietorship which is the simplest and most common form, the law does not distinguish between you and the business. You and the business are one and the same, which means your personal assets, such as your home or savings, could be at risk if the business faces debts or lawsuits. For many entrepreneurs, this structure offers simplicity and control but comes with the trade-off of personal risk.

On the other hand, forming a separate legal entity, such as a limited liability company (LLC) or corporation creates a legal shield between you and your business. These structures establish the business as an independent "person" in the eyes of the law, capable of owning assets, entering contracts, and incurring liabilities on its own. This separation is valuable because it protects your personal assets from business risks, limiting your liability to what you have invested in the company. For small business owners concerned about risk, this is often a critical consideration.

Beyond liability, the legal structure also impacts how your business is taxed. A sole proprietorship's income is reported on your personal tax return, meaning profits are taxed once as personal income. This pass-through taxation simplifies filing but may expose you to higher tax rates depending on your earnings. Corporations, by contrast, are taxed separately, potentially leading to double taxation, first on corporate profits, then on dividends paid to shareholders. However, there are variations, such as S corporations, that allow profits to pass through without corporate-level taxation, offering tax benefits for certain businesses.

Choosing the right legal structure also affects your ability to raise capital and attract investors. Corporations can issue stock, making it easier to bring in partners or outside investors. LLCs offer flexibility in ownership but generally cannot issue stock. Sole proprietorships and partnerships have more limited options for external funding, often relying on personal savings or loans. For entrepreneurs with ambitions to scale or attract investment, the legal structure must align with these goals.

Administrative complexity and cost also vary by legal structure. Sole proprietorships require minimal paperwork and are inexpensive to start, making them attractive to entrepreneurs launching a business with limited resources. LLCs and corporations, however, involve more complex formation processes, fees, and ongoing compliance requirements, such as annual reports, record-keeping, and separate tax filings. While these may seem burdensome, they also bring legitimacy and credibility to your business, which can open doors to customers, vendors, and financial institutions. Another important consideration is ownership and management flexibility. Sole proprietorships are owned and controlled by a single individual, simplifying decision-making but limiting perspectives. Partnerships allow two or more individuals to share ownership and responsibilities, which can be advantageous but also requires clear agreements to avoid conflicts. LLCs combine elements of partnerships and corporations, offering flexible management structures and profit-sharing arrangements. Corporations have more rigid governance, with boards of directors and formal shareholder meetings, which can be appropriate for businesses with multiple stakeholders.

For many small-scale entrepreneurs, the decision often comes down to balancing simplicity and protection. Starting as a sole proprietorship is common because it allows you to get up and running quickly with minimal cost. As the business grows and risks increase, many owners choose to transition to an LLC or corporation to safeguard their personal assets and position the business for future growth. This evolutionary approach allows entrepreneurs to learn and adapt their legal structure as their business matures.

It is also worth noting that the choice of legal structure can influence your credibility with customers and suppliers. Some customers, especially larger businesses or government agencies, may prefer to work with incorporated entities due to perceived stability and professionalism. Vendors might offer better terms or lines of credit to businesses with formal legal status. Even banks may require an LLC or corporation to open certain types of business accounts or approve loans. While these considerations may not be paramount at the start, they become increasingly important as you scale.

Additionally, location and industry can affect your options and requirements. Different states and countries have varying regulations, fees, and tax treatments for business structures. Certain industries may have licensing or compliance rules tied to legal structure. It is essential to research the specific laws that apply to your business and seek professional advice when necessary to ensure compliance and optimal setup. For example, a freelance graphic designer operating as a sole proprietor may enjoy the simplicity and low cost of this structure but may eventually form an LLC to protect personal assets as they take on larger projects or subcontractors. A small retail store owner might start as a sole proprietor but transition to a corporation to enable outside investment or open additional locations. Each path reflects the unique goals, risk tolerance, and resources of the entrepreneur.

Ultimately, choosing the right legal structure requires thoughtful reflection on your business goals, your tolerance for risk, your growth plans, and your willingness to manage administrative obligations. It is not a one-size-fits-all decision but a strategic foundation that supports your business's future. Taking the time to understand the implications and to seek guidance from legal or financial professionals can save headaches, protect your assets, and position your business for success. In summary, the legal structure of your business shapes the very nature of your enterprise. It influences your personal liability, taxation, funding opportunities, management flexibility, and credibility. By choosing the right legal framework, you build a strong foundation that balances simplicity and protection, enabling your small-scale business to navigate challenges and seize opportunities. This choice is a crucial step in transforming your vision into a resilient and enduring enterprise.

Behind every successful small-scale business lies an often invisible but essential element: an operational blueprint. While vision and strategy paint the picture of where the business is headed, and legal structures provide the framework for protection and compliance, operations are the engine that keeps the business running day after day. Designing an effective operational blueprint is about creating the systems, processes, and workflows that transform ideas into consistent, reliable execution. Without this foundation, even the best business model or strategy risks collapsing under the weight of inefficiency, errors, and unpredictability.

An operational blueprint is, in essence, a detailed map of how the business functions internally. It defines the sequence of activities required to produce and deliver your product or service, how resources are allocated, who is responsible for what, and what tools or technologies are needed. This blueprint addresses the question: How do you turn your business model into repeatable, scalable actions that deliver value consistently?

For many small business owners, especially those just starting, operations are informal and reactive. The owner juggles tasks, improvising daily solutions and managing workflows through memory or simple checklists. While this approach may work initially, it quickly reaches its limits as complexity grows. Customers expect consistent quality and timely delivery. Employees need clear guidance and roles. Vendors demand predictable ordering. Without a defined operational system, inefficiencies creep in such as delays, errors, miscommunications eroding profitability and customer satisfaction.

Designing an operational blueprint begins with mapping out every key process in your business. This could include sourcing materials, manufacturing or service delivery, inventory management, order fulfillment, customer support, and financial administration. Each process is broken down into clear steps, with assigned responsibilities and timelines. By documenting these workflows, you create clarity not only for yourself but for anyone involved in the business. This clarity reduces dependency on any one person and allows the business to run smoothly even in your absence.

Another vital aspect of the operational blueprint is standardization. When processes are standardized, outcomes become predictable. Customers receive the same high-quality product or service every time. Employees know exactly how to perform their tasks. Standardization also paves the way for training new staff, scaling operations, and implementing quality control measures. Without it, growth is haphazard, relying on the heroics of individuals rather than sound systems.

Operational efficiency also depends on identifying bottlenecks and waste within your processes. This might mean streamlining redundant steps, automating repetitive tasks, or reorganizing workflows to minimize delays. For example, a small catering business might optimize its ordering and preparation process to reduce food waste and ensure timely delivery. By continuously evaluating and refining operations, you make your business leaner and more responsive.

Technology plays a significant role in modern operational blueprints. From simple accounting software and inventory tracking tools to customer relationship management (CRM) systems and e-commerce platforms, technology enables small businesses to automate and scale their operations. Choosing the right tools tailored to your business needs can free up valuable time, reduce errors, and improve customer experience. However, it's important not to overcomplicate; technology should support your operations, not create new headaches.

Communication is another critical dimension of operational design. Clear, timely communication channels within your team and with customers and suppliers ensure everyone stays aligned. Regular check-ins, defined reporting structures, and transparent feedback loops prevent misunderstandings and foster a culture of accountability and continuous improvement. Even in a small business, effective communication is a powerful operational asset. An often-overlooked benefit of a well-designed operational blueprint is risk management. By anticipating potential failure points and building contingency plans, your business becomes more resilient. For example, having backup suppliers, clear quality control protocols, and documented procedures for handling customer complaints protects the business from disruption and reputational damage. This preparedness builds trust with customers and partners alike.

Designing your operational blueprint also forces you to consider capacity and scalability. How many customers can your business serve without sacrificing quality? How will you manage increased demand? What roles will you need to hire for, and when? Planning these elements early helps avoid growing pains and positions your business to seize opportunities as they arise.

Most importantly, the operational blueprint should reflect and support your business's unique value proposition and goals. For instance, if your competitive edge is exceptional customer service, your operations must prioritize responsiveness and personalized attention. If cost leadership is your strategy, efficiency and waste reduction take center stage. Operations are not just about internal mechanics; they are an expression of your brand promise. Creating and refining this blueprint requires ongoing effort and learning. The first version is rarely perfect. As your business evolves, so too must your operations. Regularly reviewing workflows, soliciting feedback from customers and employees, and staying open to innovation keep your business agile and competitive. The operational blueprint is a living document which is dynamic and responsive.

A business can have a powerful vision and a robust strategy but if these two forces move in different directions, the result is confusion, misalignment, and lost potential. Vision is your long-term picture of success, your reason for building the business in the first place. Strategy, on the other hand, is the set of actions and choices that guide you toward that vision. Aligning the two is not just about good planning, it's about making sure that every move you make, every dollar you spend, and every goal you set is in service of the future you're trying to build. Without this alignment, a business may achieve activity without progress, motion without meaning.

At the heart of alignment lies clarity. The clearer your vision, the more effectively you can craft a strategy to realize it. Vision is not just a lofty slogan or a motivational poster but it's a deep articulation of what your business stands for, who it serves, and what impact it aims to make. It is both emotional and aspirational, a standard that keeps you oriented in times of uncertainty. A strong vision answers questions like: Why does this business exist? What change do we want to create in our community, our industry, or our customers' lives?

But vision alone is not enough. Many entrepreneurs have inspiring dreams but fail to translate them into concrete, strategic steps. This is where alignment becomes critical. Strategy is the process of turning vision into action. It involves setting priorities, allocating resources, defining your unique position in the market, and deciding what you will and will not do. It's about making trade-offs, choosing focus over dilution, and crafting a roadmap that transforms purpose into progress. When your strategy flows directly from your vision, you build a business that doesn't just function but it resonates.

Misalignment between vision and strategy often shows up subtly. A business might claim to be customer-centric, but invest heavily in automation that removes human touch. It might aim to empower local artisans, but make decisions that prioritize low-cost outsourcing. These disconnects erode trust internally and externally and lead to strategies that contradict the very heart of the business. Over time, this weakens culture, dilutes brand identity, and undermines morale. Alignment, by contrast, creates integrity where your actions reflect your values, and your decisions reinforce your goals.

The process of aligning vision with strategy begins with self-awareness. As a business owner, you must deeply understand your own motivations, values, and long-term ambitions. What kind of life do you want your business to support? What kind of legacy do you want it to leave? These personal reflections form the backbone of a meaningful vision. Once this vision is clear, strategic planning becomes a matter of asking: What must happen to make this vision real? What must we build, prioritize, and protect?

Strategic alignment also requires that you continually test your assumptions. Markets shift, technologies evolve, and customer needs change. A strategy that was perfectly aligned with your vision one year may fall out of step the next. Regular reflection through planning sessions, customer feedback, and performance reviews ensures your strategy stays dynamic and responsive. This ongoing process of realignment keeps your business rooted in its purpose, even as it adapts to the world around it. Another important aspect of alignment is communication. If you have a team, they must understand and believe in the vision and see how their daily work contributes to it. Strategy becomes empowering when people understand the "why" behind the "what." When vision is shared, strategy becomes a collective pursuit rather than a top-down directive. Even if you are a solo entrepreneur, articulating your vision and strategy in writing, on paper, or in conversation helps clarify your focus and strengthen your resolve.

Alignment also brings focus. In a world full of opportunities, distractions, and trends, a clear alignment between vision and strategy acts as a filter. Not every opportunity is right for your business. Not every growth path honors your purpose. By using your vision as a lens, you can evaluate decisions not just for profitability, but for relevance and fit. This discipline helps avoid the trap of chasing short-term gains at the expense of long-term meaning.

Importantly, aligning vision with strategy empowers small businesses to differentiate. In competitive markets, your vision is often what sets you apart which includes your story, your values, your approach. A strategy grounded in that vision creates offerings and experiences that feel authentic and memorable. It builds emotional connection with customers and loyalty over time. When your business operates in harmony with its beliefs, it transcends being just a provider as it becomes a trusted part of people's lives.

This alignment also builds resilience. Businesses that are strategically aligned with a deeper vision can weather storms more effectively. They have a reason to keep going when things get tough. They have a core identity that doesn't depend on external trends. And they attract customers, partners, and employees who share their values, people who are more likely to stick with them through thick and thin. This kind of strength isn't built on spreadsheets or marketing plans, it's built on coherence between what a business says, what it believes, and what it does.

It's worth noting that alignment is not about rigidity. It doesn't mean refusing to evolve. In fact, the most aligned businesses are those that grow and innovate while remaining true to their core. They understand that vision and strategy are not static documents, but living principles. When a new opportunity arises, they ask: Does this move us closer to our vision? When a setback hits, they ask: What does this teach us about our path? This reflective approach allows them to change wisely, without losing their identity. In the end, aligning vision with strategy is a quiet but transformative practice. It elevates everyday work into meaningful progress. It gives decisions a deeper context. It fosters authenticity, clarity, and trust. For small-scale businesses, this alignment is not a luxury but it is the very fabric of sustainability. Because in a world full of noise, the businesses that endure are not just those that operate efficiently, but those that operate with purpose.

CHAPTER THREE
DESIGNING SYSTEMS THAT WORK

When people think about small-scale businesses, they often picture a passionate entrepreneur juggling many tasks at once, a storefront buzzing with customers, or a workshop where creativity flows freely. While these images capture important elements of entrepreneurship, they sometimes obscure a critical but less glamorous aspect of success: the internal processes that keep everything running smoothly behind the scenes. Internal processes are those defined sequences of activities, routines, and protocols which are the backbone of any effective business. Without them, passion and creativity can quickly get overwhelmed by chaos, inefficiency, and inconsistency.

At its core, an internal process is simply a set of repeatable steps that transform inputs into desired outputs. This might mean how a product moves from raw materials to finished goods, how customer orders are received and fulfilled, or how financial records are maintained. Although this sounds straightforward, many small businesses operate without formally defining these processes. They rely heavily on the intuition and memory of the owner or a small team, which may work initially but becomes fragile as the business grows or faces unexpected challenges.

Why do internal processes matter so much? The answer lies in their power to create consistency, efficiency, and scalability. Consistency is perhaps the most immediate benefit. Customers expect a certain standard whether it's the taste of a dish at a café, the quality of a handmade product, or the responsiveness of customer service. Internal processes ensure that these expectations are met time and time again by codifying the steps needed to deliver quality. When a process is well designed and followed, it reduces errors and variability, which means fewer unhappy customers and more repeat business.

Efficiency is another major advantage. Well-crafted processes eliminate wasted effort, minimize delays, and optimize resource use. For example, a small retailer who has a defined system for restocking shelves and managing inventory will avoid stockouts or overstock situations that tie up cash unnecessarily. Efficiency frees up time and energy, allowing the business owner and employees to focus on higher-value activities, innovation, or growth rather than putting out fires.

Scalability flows naturally from consistency and efficiency. When you have clear processes, you can train new employees faster, delegate tasks confidently, and replicate your business model in new locations or markets. Without processes, scaling is risky as the quality and reliability that made your business successful can deteriorate quickly as complexity increases. Systems create a foundation on which growth can safely rest. Internal processes also improve decision-making. By documenting how things get done, businesses gain visibility into what works well and what doesn't. This transparency allows for data-driven improvements rather than reactive guesswork. For instance, tracking the time taken to fulfill orders can highlight bottlenecks or inefficiencies that, once addressed, can dramatically improve customer satisfaction and profitability.

Another important role of internal processes is risk management. A business that relies solely on individual memory or informal communication is vulnerable to mistakes, missed deadlines, or even fraud. Defined processes include checkpoints and controls that reduce these risks, protecting the business's financial health and reputation. Having a clear approval process for expenses prevents unauthorized spending, while a standardized customer complaint handling procedure ensures issues are resolved professionally and promptly.

The human element is deeply intertwined with processes. People perform tasks, but it is the system that guides their actions, expectations, and interactions. When employees understand the processes, they feel more confident and empowered. Clear processes reduce confusion, conflict, and burnout because everyone knows their role and how it fits into the bigger picture. This clarity can be a powerful motivator, fostering a culture of accountability and continuous improvement.

Many small business owners underestimate the importance of internal processes because they confuse systems with bureaucracy or rigidity. They fear that formalizing processes will stifle creativity or flexibility. The truth is the opposite: good processes provide structure without unnecessary constraints. They create space for creativity by handling routine tasks efficiently, so the business owner can focus on innovation, customer relationships, and strategic thinking. Flexibility can be built into processes by allowing room for judgment and adaptation when needed. Creating internal processes also supports customer experience in profound ways. Behind every positive interaction, there is often a well-designed process ensuring that customers receive timely responses, accurate information, and consistent service. For instance, a well-structured process for handling online orders not only speeds up delivery but also communicates clearly to customers, reducing anxiety and building trust. These small details differentiate businesses in competitive markets.

Furthermore, internal processes help maintain compliance with laws and regulations. From tax filings and labor laws to health and safety standards, defined procedures ensure that nothing important slips through the cracks. This protects the business from legal penalties and reputational damage, which can be devastating for small enterprises.

Developing effective internal processes starts with observing how work currently gets done. Many businesses discover that the actual day-to-day operations differ from what is imagined or planned. Mapping out existing workflows, even if informal, is the first step to understanding strengths and weaknesses. Engaging employees who perform these tasks is invaluable, as they offer practical insights that can refine processes.

The next step is standardizing these workflows by documenting each step clearly and logically. This documentation becomes a reference that guides training, quality control, and continuous improvement. However, documentation should be clear and accessible, avoiding overly complex manuals that no one reads. Visual tools like flowcharts or checklists can make processes easier to understand and follow.

Once processes are defined, implementation requires training and communication. Everyone involved must understand not only what the process is but why it matters. When people see the connection between their work and the business's success, they are more likely to embrace new procedures enthusiastically. Leaders play a critical role here by modeling adherence to processes and encouraging feedback.

Importantly, processes are not static. They require regular review and refinement as the business environment changes. Customer preferences evolve, technology advances, and new challenges arise. An internal process that was effective last year may become outdated or inefficient. Building a culture of continuous improvement means encouraging experimentation, learning from mistakes, and adapting processes proactively.

Technology offers powerful opportunities to enhance internal processes. Simple tools like spreadsheets and calendars can organize workflows, while specialized software automates routine tasks and integrates different business functions. For example, inventory management systems can track stock levels in real time, alerting the owner to reorder before running out. Customer relationship management (CRM) platforms keep track of interactions and sales opportunities systematically. While technology adoption requires investment and learning, it can transform the scalability and professionalism of a small business.

It is essential to tailor internal processes to the unique needs and scale of your business. Over-engineering processes for a small operation can waste time and frustrate people. Conversely, underdeveloped processes leave the business vulnerable to chaos. Finding the right balance means starting simple, focusing on high-impact areas, and expanding gradually as the business grows.

Internal processes may not capture the romantic imagination of entrepreneurship, but they are the essential gears that keep the business clock ticking. They provide consistency, efficiency, scalability, risk management, and a framework for continuous improvement. By understanding and investing in internal processes, small-scale business owners transform their passion into a professional enterprise capable of thriving in today's dynamic markets. Designing and refining these systems is an ongoing journey which is one that rewards discipline and foresight with lasting success.

For many small-scale businesses, inventory management is a critical yet challenging aspect of daily operations. Whether you run a boutique store, a café, or a crafts workshop, keeping track of stock and supplies can make the difference between smooth sales and missed opportunities, between profit and loss. Effective inventory management is not simply about knowing what you have on the shelves but it is about having the right products, in the right quantities, at the right time, all while minimizing costs and maximizing customer satisfaction. Yet, despite its importance, many small businesses struggle with managing inventory efficiently, often due to lack of systems or overwhelming complexity. This subsection explores why inventory management matters, common pitfalls, and how to create streamlined, practical systems tailored to small-scale operations.

Inventory, in its broadest sense, includes all the goods, raw materials, and supplies a business holds for sale or use. It is both an asset and a liability as too little inventory can result in stockouts, lost sales, and unhappy customers, while too much inventory ties up valuable capital and increases storage costs. Striking the right balance is a delicate act that requires ongoing attention and smart management. For small businesses, the challenge is compounded by limited resources, unpredictable demand, and sometimes a lack of formal processes.

The first step toward streamlining inventory management is understanding its strategic role in your business. Inventory is not just about having products but it is about supporting your business's ability to meet customer needs reliably and promptly. When you consistently have what customers want, you build trust and encourage repeat business. Conversely, frequent stockouts or delays damage your reputation and give customers reasons to turn elsewhere.

At the same time, inventory management impacts your cash flow. Every item sitting unsold is money that could be invested elsewhere. This is especially critical for small businesses, where cash flow is often tight and flexibility is limited. Over-ordering can lead to excess stock that may become obsolete or expire, while under-ordering risks halting sales and disappointing customers. Effective inventory management helps you optimize purchasing decisions to maintain healthy stock levels, supporting both customer satisfaction and financial health.

One common mistake small businesses make is treating inventory management as a reactive process. Waiting until stock runs low to reorder, or ordering impulsively based on gut feelings, leads to unpredictability and stress. Instead, inventory management should be proactive, guided by data and planning. Knowing your sales patterns, lead times from suppliers, and seasonality allows you to forecast demand and plan inventory accordingly. Even small businesses can track these factors through simple tools, such as spreadsheets or basic inventory software. Another challenge is organizing inventory physically. A cluttered or disorganized storage area slows down operations, increases errors, and raises the risk of damage or loss. A well-organized space, with clearly labeled bins or shelves, and a logical layout aligned with how you access and use items, saves time and reduces frustration. Regularly reviewing your storage setup ensures it adapts to changing inventory types and volumes.

Technology can be a game-changer in inventory management. Many affordable and user-friendly inventory management software solutions exist today that cater to small businesses. These systems automate tracking, generate alerts when stock is low, and provide real-time insights into inventory status. Integration with sales platforms can streamline order fulfillment and purchasing, reducing manual errors and saving time. While adopting new technology requires an initial investment of time and learning, the long-term benefits often outweigh the costs.

Effective inventory management also hinges on establishing clear processes. Defining who is responsible for monitoring stock levels, placing orders, receiving deliveries, and conducting regular audits creates accountability and consistency. For example, setting a regular schedule to count inventory whether weekly, monthly, or quarterly helps catch discrepancies early and maintain accurate records. Without such processes, mistakes can accumulate, leading to costly errors and wasted resources.

Vendor relationships are another key component of successful inventory management. Developing strong partnerships with reliable suppliers improves lead times, enables better negotiation of prices and terms, and can provide flexibility when unexpected demand arises. Good communication with suppliers ensures you are informed about availability, delivery schedules, and any potential disruptions. In some cases, suppliers may offer consignment inventory or flexible ordering arrangements that reduce your carrying costs.

Small businesses must also consider the nature of their inventory when designing management systems. Perishable goods, such as food or cosmetics, require tight control over expiration dates and storage conditions to prevent loss. Seasonal or trend-based products demand agile planning to avoid overstocking obsolete items. Custom or made-to-order inventory models rely on different workflows, often integrating closely with production or service processes.

Training employees on inventory management practices is crucial. When team members understand why inventory control matters and how to follow procedures, errors decrease and efficiency improves. Simple steps such as scanning barcodes, recording incoming and outgoing stock accurately, and reporting discrepancies build a culture of care and responsibility around inventory. Streamlining inventory management also opens opportunities for cost savings. By analyzing sales data, businesses can identify slow-moving items to discount or phase out, freeing up space and capital. Consolidating orders or adjusting order frequency can reduce shipping costs. Regularly reviewing supplier performance and pricing helps keep procurement competitive. Ultimately, effective inventory management supports better customer experience. When customers find products available and receive orders promptly, their satisfaction increases, fostering loyalty and positive word-of-mouth. It also reduces stress and firefighting for business owners and staff, creating a smoother daily operation and more time to focus on growth and innovation.

It is a vital internal process that demands attention, planning, and systems. For small-scale businesses, streamlining inventory means balancing stock levels with demand, organizing storage efficiently, leveraging technology, establishing clear responsibilities, and building strong supplier relationships. When done well, it strengthens cash flow, boosts customer satisfaction, and forms a foundation for sustainable growth. By embracing inventory management as a strategic priority rather than an afterthought, small business owners equip themselves with a powerful tool for success.

For a small-scale business, whether it produces goods or delivers services, the way work flows from start to finish profoundly shapes customer experience, operational efficiency, and ultimately, profitability. Workflows represent the sequence of tasks and decisions that transform ideas, materials, or inputs into finished products or services delivered to customers. Crafting effective workflows is about designing these sequences thoughtfully, with clarity, purpose, and adaptability. When done right, workflows reduce errors, eliminate wasted effort, enhance quality, and empower employees. When neglected, they breed confusion, delay, frustration, and lost revenue.

At its essence, a workflow is a map of how work happens. For a product-based business, this might include sourcing materials, production steps, quality checks, packaging, and delivery. For a service business, it involves client intake, needs assessment, service delivery, follow-up, and feedback collection. Though workflows vary widely, the principles of design remain consistent: clarity, simplicity, efficiency, and alignment with customer expectations.

One of the most common challenges in small businesses is that workflows often develop informally or evolve haphazardly. This organic growth can work initially when the business is small and the owner is hands-on, but it tends to create bottlenecks and inconsistencies as demand grows or team members increase. Without clear workflows, tasks overlap or get missed, responsibilities are unclear, and the quality of outputs can vary widely. This unpredictability not only frustrates customers but also stresses the team, increasing the risk of burnout.

Designing effective workflows begins with understanding the end-to-end process clearly. This means mapping out each step involved, from the moment a customer places an order or requests a service, through every action until delivery and follow-up. It is important to capture who performs each task, what tools or resources are required, and what outputs or checkpoints occur along the way. Visual tools such as flowcharts or diagrams can be invaluable for illustrating these processes in a clear and accessible way. Clarity in workflow design also involves defining roles and responsibilities explicitly. When everyone knows what is expected of them and how their work connects to the broader process, coordination improves and errors decrease. This clarity helps prevent duplicated efforts and gaps, ensuring smooth transitions between steps. For small businesses with multiple hats worn by few people, clear role definition even if flexible helps maintain order and accountability.

Simplicity is another key principle. Workflows should be as streamlined as possible, avoiding unnecessary complexity or redundant steps. Complexity not only slows operations but also increases the likelihood of mistakes and makes training new team members harder. Wherever possible, unnecessary tasks should be eliminated or combined, and decision points should be clearly defined to avoid ambiguity.

Efficiency in workflows means designing processes to minimize wait times, reduce movement or handoffs, and optimize resource use. For example, grouping similar tasks together or sequencing steps to avoid backtracking saves time and effort. In production, this might mean setting up workstations in logical order; in services, it could involve scheduling appointments to maximize availability and reduce idle time. Efficiency also means anticipating potential bottlenecks and building in contingencies, such as backup plans when key resources are unavailable.

Alignment with customer expectations is crucial. Workflows should be designed not just for internal convenience but to deliver value and satisfaction externally. This means understanding what customers care about speed, quality, personalization, communication and embedding these priorities into the process. In a service workflow, ensuring timely follow-up communications can greatly enhance the customer experience. In production, rigorous quality checks at critical points prevent defective goods from reaching customers.

Flexibility should be built into workflows to handle variability. Small businesses often face unpredictable demand, custom orders, or last-minute changes. Workflows that are too rigid can struggle under these conditions, causing delays or errors. Designing workflows with built-in flexibility, such as decision points where employees can adapt based on circumstances, empowers teams to respond effectively without sacrificing control.

Communication is a vital element throughout workflows. Clear handoffs, standardized forms or tools, and shared information systems ensure that everyone involved has the data and context they need. In small businesses, where informal communication is common, formalizing key touchpoints helps avoid misunderstandings and ensures consistency. For instance, a service business might use a client intake form that captures essential information to guide the entire process. Training and documentation are essential to embedding effective workflows into daily operations. Even the best-designed processes falter if team members are unaware or unclear about them. Creating simple manuals, checklists, or job aids supports consistent execution and speeds up onboarding. Encouraging feedback from the team on workflow design fosters continuous improvement and greater buy-in.

Technology offers many tools to support workflows. Project management software, task tracking apps, and workflow automation tools can coordinate tasks, send reminders, and monitor progress in real time. For production businesses, digital tools can integrate inventory management with production scheduling. Service businesses benefit from CRM systems that track client interactions and automate follow-ups. However, technology should be chosen carefully to fit the business's scale and needs, avoiding over complication. Quality control is integral to workflows. Embedding checks and reviews at key stages prevents defects and service failures before they reach customers. This can be as simple as a checklist before shipment or a follow-up call after service delivery. When problems are caught early, the business saves time, money, and reputation.

Workflow design also influences business culture. Clear, efficient processes foster a sense of professionalism, reliability, and pride among team members. When employees see how their work contributes to the whole, they feel valued and motivated. Conversely, chaotic or unclear workflows breed frustration, mistakes, and turnover. In summary, crafting effective service and production workflows is a strategic investment that pays dividends in operational excellence and customer satisfaction. By mapping processes clearly, defining roles, streamlining steps, aligning with customer needs, embedding flexibility, enhancing communication, supporting with technology, and ensuring quality, small businesses can create workflows that work reliably and scale gracefully. This thoughtful approach transforms daily tasks from a source of stress into a source of strength.

In the fast-paced world of small-scale business, the difference between thriving and merely surviving often hinges on how daily tasks are managed. While big-picture strategy and long-term planning are crucial, it is the day-to-day routine, the steady rhythm of repeated actions that keeps the business moving forward. Establishing effective daily task routines is essential for boosting productivity, reducing stress, and ensuring consistency. Yet, many small business owners struggle to create routines that work for them and their teams, either because they feel overwhelmed by constant demands or because they underestimate the power of structure.

Daily task routines are not about rigid schedules that stifle creativity or spontaneity; rather, they are about creating a dependable framework that supports focus, efficiency, and progress. These routines help clarify priorities, allocate time wisely, and manage energy throughout the workday. For small businesses, where resources are often limited and multitasking is the norm, a well-designed routine transforms chaos into order.

The foundation of a productive daily routine begins with understanding the nature of the tasks that must be accomplished regularly. These include operational activities like checking inventory levels, responding to customer inquiries, processing orders, managing finances, and marketing efforts. Without a clear sense of these recurring tasks and their timing, important activities may be overlooked or delayed, causing ripple effects on the business's health. Prioritization is central to effective daily routines. Not all tasks carry equal weight, and distinguishing between urgent, important, and routine tasks allows business owners and employees to focus their efforts where they matter most. Tools such as the Eisenhower Matrix can help categorize tasks, though even simple daily to-do lists can bring clarity. Building routines around the most impactful activities ensures that time is invested in work that drives results, rather than being swallowed by distractions or minor tasks.

Time blocking is a widely recommended technique for managing daily workflows. This involves allocating specific chunks of time to particular tasks or groups of tasks, creating a structured timetable. Time blocking helps prevent the common trap of reactive work, where urgent but low-value demands consume the day. For small businesses, dedicating blocks for customer service, inventory checks, social media updates, or bookkeeping creates predictability and reduces the mental load of constant decision-making. Another important aspect is batching similar tasks together. Performing tasks of the same nature consecutively minimizes the inefficiency of switching gears repeatedly. For example, setting aside time in the morning to respond to all emails at once, rather than sporadically throughout the day, conserves focus and energy. Batching also streamlines workflows, helping employees stay "in the zone" and complete tasks faster with fewer errors.

Routine also involves building habits that support productivity. Habits such as starting the day by reviewing priorities, taking short breaks to recharge, and ending with a brief reflection or plan for the next day create a rhythm that sustains performance. Small business owners benefit from self-awareness by recognizing their own peak energy times and scheduling demanding tasks accordingly, whether early mornings or afternoons.

Communication routines are equally vital. Regular team check-ins, even brief daily stand-ups, keep everyone aligned, share updates, and identify obstacles before they escalate. In small businesses where teams often wear many hats, these touchpoints build cohesion and prevent misunderstandings. Similarly, maintaining routines for customer communication, such as daily review of inquiries or feedback, ensures responsiveness and strengthens relationships.

Flexibility is key when designing daily routines. No plan survives contact with reality perfectly, especially in small businesses where unpredictability is common. Effective routines allow for adjustment, accommodating urgent customer needs or unexpected opportunities without losing sight of core priorities. Building buffer time into schedules helps absorb surprises without derailment. Technology plays a powerful role in supporting daily routines. Calendar apps, task managers, reminders, and automation tools help track tasks and deadlines, reduce manual effort, and keep priorities visible. For example, apps like Trello or Asana enable task assignment and progress tracking, even for small teams. Setting up recurring tasks in these systems ensures that routine activities aren't forgotten amidst busyness.

Avoiding burnout is another critical benefit of good daily routines. The demands of small business ownership often push owners and staff to work long hours under pressure. Structured routines that balance work with breaks, time for learning, and personal care sustain long-term productivity and wellbeing. Encouraging a culture where routine includes self-care signals respect for the team's health and fosters resilience.

Measuring the effectiveness of daily routines is important to ensure continuous improvement. Reflecting on what tasks were accomplished, what took longer than expected, and where bottlenecks occurred helps refine routines over time. Small business owners can use simple journaling or team feedback sessions to evaluate and adjust workflows, building routines that evolve with the business's changing needs. Moreover, daily task routines contribute to creating a professional image externally. When a business operates smoothly day in and day out, customers notice reliability and competence. Timely responses, consistent product availability, and well-managed services reflect the invisible discipline of good routines, building trust and loyalty.

Building daily task routines is not just about ticking boxes; it is about designing a sustainable work rhythm that enables focus, efficiency, and growth. Small-scale businesses that invest time and thought into their daily routines equip themselves to handle complexity, reduce stress, and deliver consistent value. These routines are the heartbeat of operational excellence and a steady pulse that carries the business forward, day after day.

For any small-scale business striving for long-term success, setting up internal processes is only the beginning. The true key to sustained growth and operational excellence lies in monitoring those processes and continuously seeking ways to improve them. Processes that worked well last year or even last month can become outdated or inefficient as the business evolves, customer demands shift, or new technologies emerge. Continuous monitoring and improvement create a dynamic environment where a business not only survives but thrives, adapting to change with agility and foresight.

Monitoring internal processes begins with establishing clear metrics and indicators that reflect how well each process performs. This means identifying what success looks like and how it can be measured. For example, in inventory management, key indicators might include stock turnover rates, frequency of stockouts, or order accuracy. For service workflows, customer satisfaction scores, turnaround times, or repeat business rates might serve as valuable benchmarks. Defining these metrics allows business owners and managers to move beyond gut feelings and anecdotal evidence, instead relying on concrete data to guide decisions.

Small businesses often face challenges in collecting and analyzing process data due to limited resources or lack of formal systems. However, even simple tools such as spreadsheets, checklists, or basic software can provide meaningful insights. The critical factor is consistency which involves regularly gathering data to track trends and spot issues before they escalate. This discipline helps catch inefficiencies early and enables timely corrective actions. Another cornerstone of process monitoring is feedback both from customers and employees. Customers provide frontline perspectives on product quality, service responsiveness, and overall satisfaction. Encouraging honest feedback through surveys, reviews, or direct communication channels gives businesses real-world input that can pinpoint strengths and weaknesses. Meanwhile, employees engaged in day-to-day operations offer invaluable insights into process bottlenecks, redundant tasks, or opportunities for simplification. Creating a culture where feedback is welcomed and acted upon fosters collaboration and continuous improvement.

Once processes are monitored, the focus shifts to improvement. This is not a one-time event but an ongoing commitment to refine and optimize workflows. Small changes such as rearranging a workstation, automating a manual task, or revising a communication template can accumulate to produce significant efficiency gains and quality enhancements. The philosophy of incremental improvement, often known as Kaizen, emphasizes that even small, consistent tweaks contribute to long-term excellence. Problem-solving techniques play a key role in process improvement. Tools such as root cause analysis help identify underlying issues rather than superficial symptoms. For instance, if order fulfillment delays are frequent, exploring whether the cause lies in inventory shortages, communication gaps, or staffing challenges leads to targeted solutions rather than quick fixes. Small businesses benefit from adopting structured approaches to problem-solving that encourage systematic thinking and prevent recurring problems.

Technology adoption is a vital lever for improvement. As digital tools become increasingly accessible and affordable, small businesses can leverage software to automate repetitive tasks, streamline communication, and enhance data visibility. For example, integrating inventory management with sales and accounting systems reduces manual reconciliation, saves time, and minimizes errors. Similarly, customer relationship management (CRM) systems enable personalized communication and better tracking of client interactions. Continually evaluating and updating technology stacks ensures that processes stay efficient and aligned with current capabilities.

Training and capacity building underpin successful process improvement. As workflows evolve, team members need the knowledge and skills to adapt. Investing in regular training sessions, workshops, or peer learning creates an empowered workforce capable of embracing change and driving innovation. Leadership plays a pivotal role here by modeling openness to feedback and fostering an environment that rewards creativity and experimentation.

Documentation is another essential component. Clearly recorded processes, updated regularly, serve as the blueprint for consistent execution and ease onboarding. When improvements are made, documenting changes prevents regression to old habits and facilitates knowledge sharing across the team. In small businesses where informal communication is common, formal documentation elevates professionalism and operational stability. Monitoring and improving processes also support risk management. Identifying vulnerabilities such as dependence on a single supplier, manual data entry errors, or inconsistent quality checks allows businesses to implement safeguards. For example, establishing backup suppliers, adopting error-proofing techniques, or standardizing quality control can mitigate risks that threaten continuity and reputation.

One of the greatest benefits of continuous process improvement is enhanced customer experience. Streamlined operations reduce errors, speed delivery, and increase reliability. Customers notice when a business responds swiftly to their needs, resolves issues proactively, and maintains high standards. This builds trust and fosters loyalty, key drivers of sustained revenue and positive word-of-mouth. Furthermore, improved internal processes create space for growth and innovation. When daily operations run smoothly, business owners and teams can focus on strategic initiatives, exploring new markets, developing products, or enhancing marketing. The energy once spent on firefighting is redirected toward value creation, positioning the business for scalability.

It is important to recognize that process improvement is a journey, not a destination. The business environment is dynamic as customer preferences shift, technologies advance, regulations change and processes must evolve accordingly. Regularly scheduled process reviews ensure that the business remains responsive and competitive. Many successful small businesses establish quarterly or annual evaluations as part of their operational calendar.

Equally vital is fostering a mindset that views change positively rather than as disruption. Small businesses with cultures open to experimentation and learning tend to adapt more quickly and outperform those resistant to change. Celebrating small wins in process improvements motivates teams and reinforces the value of continuous effort.

Monitoring and improving internal processes is an indispensable discipline for small-scale businesses seeking resilience, efficiency, and growth. By setting measurable goals, gathering data consistently, encouraging feedback, embracing technology, investing in training, and fostering a culture of continuous improvement, businesses turn routine operations into a strategic advantage. This proactive approach ensures that internal workflows remain aligned with business objectives and customer expectations, paving the way for sustained success in a competitive landscape.

CHAPTER FOUR
CUSTOMER MANAGEMENT

In the early days of running a small business, it's common to focus energy on making the sale. After all, sales bring cash, validate your product or service, and keep your doors open. But as any seasoned entrepreneur learns, the heartbeat of sustainable success lies not just in winning the customer but in keeping them. This understanding marks a fundamental shift: from seeing each sale as an isolated transaction to viewing it as the beginning of an ongoing relationship. It is this relationship-oriented mindset that separates short-lived ventures from businesses that thrive and endure.

The transactional model of business where the focus is on the immediate exchange of money for goods or services can be appealing in its simplicity. The goal is clear: sell as much as possible, as quickly as possible. But this model is short-sighted. It treats customers as faceless units of revenue, rather than as individuals with evolving needs, preferences, and the potential for long-term engagement. While transactions are necessary, they are not sufficient.

If a customer buys from you once and never returns, your business must constantly chase new leads to survive. This approach is both exhausting and inefficient.

The relationship model, by contrast, sees each interaction as a thread in a longer narrative. In this model, the goal is not just to sell, but to connect, to serve and to understand. Each customer is not just a number but a part of a growing community around your brand. When you build relationships, you build trust and with trust comes loyalty, repeat business, and advocacy. It is far more cost-effective to retain a customer than to acquire a new one. And in the age of social media and digital word-of-mouth, satisfied customers often become your most powerful marketing force.

Shifting toward relationship-oriented thinking requires a change in perspective. It means looking at the customer journey holistically, not just what happens at the cash register, but what happens before, during, and after the sale. It means understanding how customers find you, what influences their decisions, how they experience your service, and how they feel long after the transaction is complete. Every step along this journey offers opportunities to deepen the relationship or to lose it. Trust is the cornerstone of this relationship. Customers return to businesses they trust. That trust is built through consistency, transparency, and authenticity. It begins with clear and honest communication about your products, your prices, your policies and continues with delivering on your promises. When a customer knows they can rely on you, even in small ways, you begin to earn their loyalty. And loyalty is not just about repeated purchases; it's about emotional alignment. Loyal customers believe in your brand, they defend it, and they recommend it to others.

Empathy plays a vital role in relationship-building. When you genuinely care about your customers and not just what they buy, but who they are, you create emotional resonance. Listening to their needs, responding with patience, and being flexible in solving their problems all signal that you value them as people, not just sources of income. This sense of being seen and heard can be incredibly powerful. In an increasingly impersonal world, personalized service stands out.

Small businesses have a natural advantage here. Unlike large corporations, which often rely on automated systems and distant customer service departments, small businesses can offer intimacy, warmth, and personal attention. Knowing a customer's name, remembering their preferences, asking about their family or their goals, these seemingly small gestures carry tremendous weight. They humanize the business and create a sense of belonging. Customers don't just buy a product; they buy an experience and an emotional connection.

Yet, building customer relationships does not mean saying yes to everything or compromising your boundaries. Part of building trust is being clear about what you can and cannot offer, setting expectations honestly, and standing by your values. Customers respect businesses that are confident in their identity and consistent in their behavior. It's not about pleasing everyone; it's about being authentic and dependable for your right-fit customers.

Understanding customer relationships also requires recognizing the role of emotions in purchasing decisions. While logic plays a part, buying is often deeply emotional. People choose businesses that make them feel good, safe, understood, or empowered. They remember how they were treated, how smoothly the experience went, and how they felt after the interaction. These emotional impressions linger far longer than product specifications or prices. Relationship-based businesses focus on creating positive emotional footprints in every customer touchpoint.

Moreover, relationships are not static. They evolve. A new customer has different needs and expectations than a long-term loyal client. Relationship-focused businesses adapt their approach over time, offering different forms of value depending on where the customer is in their journey. For instance, new customers may need more education and guidance, while returning customers may appreciate exclusives, loyalty rewards, or recognition. By tuning into this evolution, businesses can nurture relationships in a way that feels responsive and respectful.

Technology can assist in managing and deepening customer relationships, but it should never replace the human element. Customer relationship management (CRM) systems can track interactions, record preferences, and schedule follow-ups. Email marketing tools can personalize messages and deliver timely offers. Social media platforms can create two-way conversations and community engagement. But the heart of a customer relationship remains human. The smile, the tone of voice, the handwritten thank-you note, the genuine apology when things go wrong, all these are the moments that build or break trust.

Feedback loops are also essential. Asking for customer input, acknowledging it, and acting on it shows that you care about their experience and are committed to improvement. Regularly reviewing customer feedback whether it comes through surveys, reviews, or informal conversations helps you identify patterns, spot problems early, and discover new opportunities to serve your market better.

There is also a moral dimension to relationship-based business. When you build relationships rather than chase transactions, you are practicing a form of ethical entrepreneurship. You are committing to serve, to support, and to deliver value beyond mere profit. This creates a virtuous cycle: customers reward ethical behavior with loyalty, and loyal customers sustain the business financially and emotionally. Finally, relationship thinking is about playing the long game. It is about patience, consistency, and care. Results may not be immediate, but they are enduring. Relationships take time to build but can last a lifetime. And in a world increasingly saturated with noise and choice, genuine relationships become a differentiator that no competitor can replicate.

Moving beyond the point of sale requires a shift from transactional to relational thinking. It means seeing customers not just as buyers but as partners in a shared journey. It involves empathy, trust, communication, and the willingness to invest in long-term connection. For small-scale businesses, this approach is not only more fulfilling as it is more effective. It transforms fleeting interactions into enduring loyalty and turns every customer experience into an opportunity to build something meaningful.

In today's digitally driven marketplace, understanding your customers has become both an art and a science. While intuition and experience still play vital roles, small businesses must also harness the power of data to build and sustain meaningful customer relationships. Capturing the right customer data and using it wisely is foundational to moving beyond one-off transactions and cultivating deep, trust-based connections. It is not about spying or manipulation. It is about listening carefully, learning thoughtfully, and responding intelligently to what your customers actually need, want, and value.

Many small business owners shy away from customer data, seeing it as something complex, expensive, or reserved for large corporations with big marketing departments. But in truth, capturing and using customer data can be simple, ethical, and profoundly effective even for the smallest business. It begins with a mindset shift: recognizing that every interaction with a customer is an opportunity to learn, and that this learning, when organized and applied, can transform how you serve, engage, and retain your customer base.

The most basic and vital kind of customer data is contact information. Names, phone numbers, email addresses, and social media handles form the backbone of any customer relationship management system. This data enables communication and follow-up, allowing you to continue the conversation after the initial sale. Yet even this seemingly simple task is often overlooked by small businesses that do not have systems in place to consistently collect and store such information. Building a reliable database even if it starts as a spreadsheet creates a powerful platform for future relationship-building efforts.

Beyond basic contact details, behavioral data provides insights into how customers interact with your business. What products do they browse or purchase? How frequently do they buy? What time of year do they engage most? Which services are most popular? This kind of data, gathered through sales records, website analytics, or point-of-sale systems, helps identify patterns that inform smarter business decisions. It shows what resonates, what needs improvement, and what opportunities might exist for upselling, cross-selling, or customization.

Another critical layer of data is preference information. This includes individual tastes, needs, and desires that personalize the customer experience. For instance, a bakery might track dietary preferences (gluten-free, vegan), while a hair salon might note preferred styles, color treatments, or products. Capturing these small but significant details enables the business to anticipate needs, surprise customers with thoughtful touches, and create a sense of being known. These details turn a generic service into a tailored experience, one that is far more likely to earn loyalty.

Demographic and psychographic data add further depth. Knowing the age, occupation, lifestyle, and values of your customer base allows for more targeted communication and marketing. For example, a business targeting young professionals might use Instagram and text alerts, while one serving retirees might focus more on email or in-person updates. Psychographics, interests, attitudes, motivations help you connect on a deeper emotional level, aligning your brand messaging with what truly matters to your customers.

Crucially, the collection of customer data must always be rooted in consent, transparency, and security. Customers need to know what data you're collecting, why you're collecting it, and how it will be used. This builds trust and ensures compliance with privacy regulations such as GDPR or other local laws. A simple privacy notice, clear opt-in mechanisms, and secure data storage practices show that you respect your customers and value their information.

In a world increasingly aware of data misuse, ethical data handling becomes a competitive advantage.

Once data is captured, the next challenge is organizing it effectively. This is where customer relationship management (CRM) tools become useful. There are many accessible and affordable CRM platforms tailored for small businesses, such as HubSpot, Zoho, or even simplified systems like Mailchimp or Google Contacts. These tools help you keep track of interactions, set reminders for follow-ups, segment your audience, and automate personalized messages. Even a well-maintained spreadsheet, with columns for key customer insights, can provide a solid foundation.

The goal of organizing customer data is not to collect information for its own sake, but to enable action. When used wisely, data becomes the basis for personalization. A business might send birthday greetings with a special offer, recommend products based on past purchases, or check in with a service client after a set interval. These touches demonstrate care and attentiveness, turning occasional buyers into regulars, and regulars into raving fans.

It's also worth noting that not all valuable customer data is quantitative. Qualitative data such as stories, comments, and open-ended feedback offers rich context that numbers alone cannot. A customer telling you why they prefer one product over another, or how your service made a difference in their life, provides insight into values, emotions, and experiences that shape loyalty. Encouraging these conversations, and documenting them thoughtfully, deepens your understanding of what truly drives customer satisfaction.

Capturing and analyzing data also supports better decision-making at the strategic level. If you know that a particular segment of your audience is highly responsive to a certain promotion or product, you can tailor future efforts accordingly. If feedback consistently highlights a pain point in your service process, you can prioritize improvements that directly affect customer happiness. This data-driven approach aligns your business decisions with real-world needs, reducing guesswork and increasing impact. Moreover, as your business grows, having structured customer data makes it easier to scale. Training new staff, launching new products, or expanding into new markets becomes more efficient when you have clear records of who your customers are and how they behave. You're not starting from scratch as you're building on a solid base of knowledge that has been cultivated over time.

At its core, capturing customer data is about listening. It's about paying attention to the signals your customers are sending, whether through their actions, their words, or their silence. It's about being curious, respectful, and attentive to the relationship. This listening mindset transforms data from something dry and technical into something deeply human and a tool for empathy, connection, and service. In conclusion, customer data is not just a technical asset; it is the lifeblood of relationship-driven business. When captured ethically and used wisely, it allows small businesses to understand their customers more deeply, communicate more effectively, and serve more personally. It lays the groundwork for trust, loyalty, and long-term success. And most importantly, it honors the relationship at the heart of every transaction as the relationship between you and the customer who chose to believe in your business.

Communication is the living thread that ties a business to its customers. It's more than marketing slogans or transactional emails. It's the voice, tone, rhythm, and intention behind every message a customer receives, reads, or hears. In the context of small-scale business, where relationships are personal and trust is paramount, purposeful communication becomes one of the most powerful tools for creating loyalty and connection. It shapes not only how customers perceive your brand, but also how they feel about interacting with it.

In many businesses, communication is often reactive or automated, designed to serve immediate needs: a receipt, a shipping notification, a reply to a question. These touchpoints are important, but they barely scratch the surface of what communication can and should do. Purposeful communication goes further. It anticipates, it listens, it engages. It turns every message into a moment of affirmation, alignment, and value. When communication is handled with intention, it builds bridges not just transactions.

The first and most fundamental principle of meaningful communication is clarity. Customers want to understand what you're offering, how it works, what it costs, and what they can expect. Confusing language, hidden fees, vague policies, or misleading claims erode trust and trigger frustration. Clear communication, on the other hand, creates a sense of safety and professionalism. It shows that you respect your customers' time and intelligence. Whether you're writing website copy, product descriptions, invoices, or social media posts, clarity should be your constant goal.

But clarity alone is not enough. Effective communication must also feel personal. This is where small businesses have a tremendous advantage. Without layers of bureaucracy or impersonal systems, small businesses can speak with warmth, familiarity, and authenticity. A handwritten note in a package, a follow-up call after a service, a personalized email that reflects a customer's history and these gestures tell the customer, "We see you. We value you." And in an era where so many interactions are robotic, that kind of genuine communication stands out.

Tone matters immensely. It sets the emotional temperature of every interaction. Is your tone welcoming or rushed? Warm or cold? Confident or defensive? Customers pick up on these cues, even if only subconsciously. A friendly, conversational tone that is still professional strikes a balance that most customers appreciate. It shows that you're approachable, while also signaling that you know what you're doing. Consistency in tone across platforms such as email, social media, in-store conversations builds a coherent and trustworthy brand voice.

Timeliness is another cornerstone of purposeful communication. A well-crafted message that arrives too late loses its value. A question left unanswered, an issue unacknowledged, or a thank-you delayed can all signal disinterest or disorganization. Small businesses, with their lean structures and direct lines to customers, are uniquely positioned to respond quickly and meaningfully. Timely replies, proactive updates, and regular check-ins show that you care and caring is the root of all good communication.

Communication should also be two-way. Too often, businesses focus solely on broadcasting their message: their offers, their values, their updates. But listening is just as important as speaking. Inviting feedback, asking questions, and genuinely considering customer input transforms communication into dialogue. This not only improves your service but it deepens trust. When customers feel heard, they feel respected. And respect is the foundation of every lasting relationship.

The mediums through which you communicate matter as well. Some customers prefer emails; others respond better to texts, phone calls, or social media messages. Knowing your audience allows you to choose the right channel for the right message. For example, a formal invoice might arrive via email, while a quick update about a delayed order might be more effectively handled via text. Social media, meanwhile, offers a space for more casual, community-building communication, sharing behind-the-scenes glimpses, celebrating customer milestones, or simply showing your business's human side.

Automation can be a useful ally when used wisely. Automated emails confirming purchases, sending appointment reminders, or following up after service can improve efficiency and consistency. But automation should never replace the human touch where it matters most. A system-generated message should still feel like it came from a real person, not a robot. Avoid jargon, personalize where possible, and always provide easy ways for customers to reach a real human if needed. Automation should support the relationship, not distance it. Purposeful communication also means knowing what not to say. Over-communication can overwhelm, annoy, or desensitize customers. If every message is a sales pitch or a promotion, customers may tune out. Communication should offer value, information, inspiration, support, or encouragement. Think about what your customer needs to hear, not just what you want to say. This value-first mindset transforms your communication into a service in itself.

Crucially, communication plays a key role in managing problems and repairing trust. No matter how careful a business is, mistakes will happen. Orders get delayed, products malfunction, misunderstandings arise. In these moments, communication is not just important but it is decisive. A prompt, sincere apology, a clear explanation, and a plan to make things right can turn an upset customer into a loyal advocate. Silence, excuses, or defensiveness, on the other hand, almost always worsen the damage. Honest, humble, and accountable communication is the fastest path to rebuilding goodwill.

Storytelling is another powerful form of communication. People remember stories far more than they remember data or slogans. Sharing your journey as a business, your mission, the people behind your product, or the impact you're making in your community makes your brand relatable and human. Customers don't just want to buy, they want to belong. They want to be part of a story that matters. Storytelling invites them into that narrative and makes them feel included.

Small businesses can also use communication to educate. Informing customers about how to use a product, the philosophy behind a service, or industry trends that affect them positions the business as a trusted guide. Educational content whether blog posts, videos, workshops, or simple in-person explanations adds value and builds authority. It says, "We're not just here to sell. We're here to help." Finally, great communication must be aligned with your core values. If you claim to be eco-friendly, inclusive, community-focused, or customer-first, your words must reflect that consistently. When communication aligns with action, it reinforces authenticity. When there's a mismatch, customers notice and credibility suffers. Let your values shine through in your tone, your topics, and your transparency.

Crafting meaningful customer interactions through purposeful communication is not just a best practice but it's a business philosophy. It is how trust is built, how loyalty is earned, and how a brand comes alive in the hearts of its customers. In every email, every phone call, every message, there is a chance to show customers who you are and how much you care. And in the crowded, noisy marketplace of today, that kind of communication doesn't just get noticed and it gets remembered.

Every small business has a moment of truth which is the moment when a promise meets performance. It's when a customer walks through the door, opens the package, makes a complaint, or returns for a second visit. In these moments, what matters more than branding, marketing, or even price is this: did the business deliver the same quality of service as last time or better? Consistency is not glamorous. It's not flashy. But it is the invisible engine of trust, and trust is the most valuable currency a business can earn.

Delivering consistent service is one of the most effective ways to foster loyalty and long-term customer relationships. It tells your customers that you are dependable, that you care about their experience, and that they can count on you time and time again. When service is erratic, customers are left guessing and in that uncertainty, trust begins to erode. But when every interaction is handled with the same attention, professionalism, and warmth, a deep sense of security forms. Customers stop shopping around. They know what they'll get with you, and they like it.

Small businesses often pride themselves on personalized service and rightly so. But personalization does not mean improvisation. The most effective small businesses strike a balance between flexibility and structure. They tailor the experience to the individual customer while ensuring that certain non-negotiables such as politeness, promptness, product quality, and professionalism are consistently delivered across the board. This blend of human warmth and process-driven reliability is what sets a strong business apart.

Creating consistency starts with systems. Every task, from how a phone call is answered to how a product is packaged or a service is executed, benefits from having a clear process. These processes don't need to be rigid scripts. They can and should allow for human judgment. But they serve as a foundation that ensures nothing essential falls through the cracks. A small café, for instance, might have a checklist for closing the shop, a routine for how every coffee is served, and a clear approach to handling customer complaints. These small systems add up to a consistent customer experience.

Training is another critical component. Often, inconsistency arises not from bad intentions but from unclear expectations. When staffs don't know what "excellent service" looks like in your business, they each improvise their own version. This leads to variability, confusion, and frustration for customers and employees alike. By investing time in onboarding, shadowing, role-playing, and check-ins, you equip your team to deliver service that reflects your values and meets your standards. And when team members are confident in what's expected, they perform with greater assurance and pride.

Consistency also requires internal alignment. Every part of your operation must work together to support the customer experience. If your marketing promises same-day service but your fulfillment team can't deliver it, trust is broken. If your sales staff overpromise or misinform, and your support staff must pick up the pieces, morale suffers. This is why internal communication, regular team meetings, and cross-functional collaboration matter. A consistent external experience depends on a cohesive internal one.

Another often-overlooked aspect of consistent service is emotional consistency. Customers don't just remember what you did; they remember how you made them feel. If one visit they're greeted with enthusiasm and the next with indifference, it sends mixed signals. It makes the brand feel unstable. Small businesses can't afford to be emotionally unpredictable. Cultivating a culture of positivity, empathy, and attentiveness day in and day out goes a long way in making customers feel safe and valued.

Consistency also means handling problems with the same integrity each time. A customer who sees that mistakes are addressed fairly and consistently across the board is more likely to forgive and return. When policies are applied arbitrarily or unfairly, one customer gets a refund, another doesn't, resentment builds. Having clear, written policies for returns, complaints, or cancellations creates transparency and prevents misunderstandings. It also empowers staff to resolve issues with confidence and compassion.

While some may argue that small businesses can't afford to standardize, the truth is that they can't afford not to. Standardization doesn't strip away individuality; it creates a dependable baseline. Within that baseline, there's room for creativity, intuition, and personal flair. A consistent brand voice, look and feel, level of service, and customer interaction helps customers recognize and remember your business. Over time, this builds a brand identity that is distinct and trustworthy. Customer expectations are shaped by their previous experiences. If you went out of your way last time but fall short the next, the inconsistency stands out. Reliability becomes the lens through which everything else is judged. This is particularly important in businesses that operate on repeat visits or ongoing services such as salons, cafés, coaching, repairs, and deliveries. Inconsistency not only disappoints, it creates doubt. And doubt is the beginning of lost loyalty.

It's also important to recognize that consistent service is a team effort. It's not just about what the owner does or says. Every touchpoint whether it's the receptionist, the technician, the delivery driver, or the person managing the social media page contributes to the overall impression. Everyone must understand their role in delivering a consistent experience. This requires leadership, communication, and a shared commitment to excellence. Ironically, one of the best ways to keep service consistent is to continually assess and improve it. Regularly gather feedback from customers. Ask what's working and what's not. Observe how your team interacts with clients. Look for small ways to fine-tune your systems, simplify your processes, and close any gaps in the customer experience. Service consistency is not a one-time achievement as it's a moving target that must be maintained through vigilance and care.

Consistency doesn't mean sameness. It means dependability. It means that whether your customer comes in on Monday morning or Saturday night, they feel seen, respected, and served at the same high standard. It means that your brand feels solid, even if it's delivered by different people, across different channels, or at different times. This kind of dependability becomes a comfort to your customers and a reason to come back, to trust you again, to recommend you to others.

In a world where businesses rise and fall quickly, where customer attention is fragmented and choices are endless, the quiet power of consistent service should not be underestimated. It doesn't create headlines, but it creates habits. It doesn't go viral, but it creates loyalty. And in the long run, it is one of the most profitable and sustainable strategies any small business can adopt.

Consistency in service is not about perfection rather it's about dependability. It's about building routines and systems that support your values, training a team that understands your vision, and creating an environment where customers know what to expect and are delighted every time. In this dependable rhythm of care, attention, and reliability, trust takes root. And with trust, your business doesn't just survive but it flourishes.

In the lifecycle of a customer relationship, the transaction is only the beginning. While many businesses pour energy into attracting new buyers, the most resilient and profitable small enterprises understand that true success lies in what happens after the sale. It's not just about creating satisfied customers; it's about cultivating loyal ones. And more than that, it's about turning those loyal customers into vocal advocates who voluntarily spread the word, defend your brand, and help build your community from the inside out.

Loyalty is not a random occurrence; it's a cultivated response to consistent, meaningful experiences. Customers return to businesses where they feel valued, understood, and appreciated not simply because of the product or service, but because of the emotional relationship they've formed with the brand. Retention, then, is the art of continuing to earn that relationship over time. It's not passive as it's intentional, strategic, and deeply human.

The first step in nurturing loyalty is to show gratitude. Gratitude is not a campaign or a discount code but it's a culture. It's the way you acknowledge your customers, remember their preferences, and say "thank you" not because you have to, but because you mean it. In a world of automated messages and faceless transactions, authentic appreciation stands out. Whether it's a handwritten thank-you note, a follow-up call after a big purchase, or a small gift for a repeat customer, these gestures communicate that you see the customer as more than just revenue but they are a part of your business's story.

Retention is further supported by reliability. Customers who know they can count on you every time are far more likely to return. When you fulfill your promises, resolve issues quickly, and maintain a high standard of service, you make it easy for customers to stay. People tend to stick with brands that reduce friction in their lives. Your job is to make that decision a no-brainer by consistently exceeding expectations and removing reasons to look elsewhere.

Another powerful tool in retention is exclusivity. When customers feel they are part of an "inner circle," they are more likely to remain loyal. This doesn't have to be complicated such as a loyalty program, early access to new products, special events, or personalized offers can all create a sense of belonging. These programs tell your customers, "You matter. You're not just another sale but you're part of this." And people tend to fight for the things they feel part of.

Importantly, loyalty is also nurtured through memory. When you remember your customers, their names, their preferences, their stories, you humanize the business and deepen the connection. This is where a well-kept CRM or even simple customer notes can be incredibly effective. The ability to recall a detail from a past interaction signals attentiveness and care. It transforms a transaction into a relationship.

Education is another tool for deepening loyalty. By helping customers get more out of your products or services, you increase the value they receive, which increases their satisfaction. Tutorials, tips, workshops, blog posts, or even brief conversations that teach or guide the customer reinforce your role not just as a seller, but as a trusted partner. A customer who feels empowered by your business is one who is far more likely to return and to tell others.

When customers do return, it's essential to reward that behavior not just with perks, but with recognition. Loyalty programs that simply tally up purchases and spit out discounts miss a deeper opportunity. Recognition through shout-outs, birthday wishes, or unexpected tokens of appreciation goes further. It builds emotional equity. It says, "We see you. We remember. You're not just a number to us."

This kind of acknowledgment can mean more than any points-based incentive.

But loyalty isn't always smooth. At some point, even your best customers will experience a hiccup such as a late delivery, a miscommunication, a service that didn't go quite right. These are not failures; they're tests. And how you handle them determines whether the relationship grows or fades. Quick, empathetic responses, fair solutions, and proactive follow-up turn problems into opportunities for deepening trust. In many cases, a well-handled complaint creates a more loyal customer than one who's never had a problem at all. Over time, the most loyal customers don't just buy again, they advocate. They recommend your business to friends, leave glowing reviews, tag you on social media, and defend you in public conversations. These are the customers who help you grow without paid advertising. But advocacy doesn't happen by accident as it grows out of satisfaction, trust, and emotional investment. If you want advocates, you must first create reasons to be advocated for.

To encourage advocacy, make it easy. Ask for reviews. Create shareable content. Host events or online forums where customers can engage. Feature customer stories in your marketing. When people feel seen and included, they naturally want to share their positive experiences. But it must be genuine. You can't bribe or force advocacy as it must emerge from authentic appreciation. Give your customers reasons to talk about you, and they will. And don't overlook the power of community. When customers see that your business brings people together, they begin to feel not just loyal to you but connected to each other. Small businesses can foster this by hosting gatherings, creating online groups, collaborating with local artists or entrepreneurs, or simply highlighting their customers' achievements. Community breeds loyalty because it creates a sense of shared identity. It transforms "I buy from them" into "I belong with them."

Nurturing loyalty and retention is about depth, not volume. It's not about chasing every potential lead but about honoring the customers you already have. It's about looking beyond short-term wins to long-term relationships. Each repeat customer, each advocate, is a pillar of your business. And as those pillars grow stronger, your foundation becomes unshakable.

CHAPTER FIVE
FINANCIAL LITERACY FOR THE SMALL BUSINESS OWNER

For many small business owners, financial statements can feel like a foreign language. The jargon, the columns of numbers, the jargon-filled reports, all these can seem overwhelming, abstract, or even intimidating. Yet, at the core of every thriving business is a simple, universal truth: you cannot manage what you do not understand. And the heartbeat of that understanding lies in mastering your profit and loss often called the P&L, or income statement.

The profit and loss statement is more than just a document; it's the story of your business's financial performance over a specific period. It shows what came in, what went out, and what was left at the end of the day, or month, or quarter. Think of it as a scoreboard that tells you whether your business is winning, losing, or holding steady. But unlike a simple scoreboard in a game, the P&L offers insights that can guide your decisions, steer your strategy, and ultimately decide your business's future.

To truly grasp the profit and loss, you must start by understanding its core components. At the top is your revenue which is the total money your business has earned from selling products or services. This is the "gross" figure before any expenses are deducted. Many business owners focus heavily on revenue, and understandably so, since it feels like the primary marker of success. More sales equal more money, right? But this is only part of the story.

The next key piece is the cost of goods sold (COGS) or cost of services, which includes the direct costs related to producing your product or delivering your service. This might be raw materials, labor specifically tied to production, or other expenses directly connected to creating what you sell. Deducting these costs from your revenue gives you the gross profit which is the money left over after the cost of delivering your goods or services are covered.

Gross profit is crucial because it reveals whether your pricing and production methods are fundamentally sound. If your COGS are too high, your gross profit shrinks, meaning you're barely making enough to cover even your basic costs. Understanding this helps identify whether you need to adjust pricing, negotiate better supplier deals, or improve operational efficiencies.

Below gross profit come the operating expenses which are those necessary costs that keep your business running day-to-day but aren't directly tied to producing goods or services. These include rent, utilities, salaries for administrative staff, marketing, insurance, office supplies, and more. These expenses are the backbone of your business infrastructure, but they need to be carefully managed. When operating expenses outpace your gross profit, your business runs at a loss, no matter how strong your revenue might be. Subtracting operating expenses from gross profit results in your operating income which is a clear indicator of your core business profitability. This figure shows the profitability of your main business activities before considering other factors like taxes or interest.

Finally, you factor in any non-operating items such as interest expenses on loans, taxes, or one-time costs or gains, which leads you to your net profit or net loss, the bottom line. This figure tells you, unequivocally, whether your business made money or lost money during the period.

Many entrepreneurs focus heavily on revenue growth, but failing to understand the implications of expenses often leads to the dangerous illusion of profitability. A business can have soaring sales but still be losing money if its costs spiral out of control. This is why the profit and loss statement is not just about celebration but it's a tool for honest assessment, hard decisions, and strategic planning.

Understanding the P&L also helps with forecasting and budgeting. When you know your typical expenses and how they fluctuate, you can better predict how much revenue you need to break even or achieve your profit goals. It allows you to set realistic targets and monitor progress regularly. Without this, businesses drift, reacting to problems only after they become crises. It is important to realize that the P&L tells a story over a specific time frame as it's a snapshot, not a complete picture. To get a fuller understanding, it should be read alongside your balance sheet (which shows what your business owns and owes at a point in time) and your cash flow statement (which we'll cover in later chapters). Together, these reports give a comprehensive view of your financial health.

A common mistake small business owners make is mixing personal and business finances, which can distort the P&L and make true profitability impossible to gauge. Keeping clear boundaries helps ensure your financial statements reflect only the business's reality.

Finally, remember that your P&L is a living document. Review it regularly, not just when tax season rolls around. Make it part of your routine to examine revenues, expenses, and profits, and ask yourself: What is this number telling me? Are my costs creeping up unnoticed? Is one product or service dragging down profits? Are there opportunities to improve efficiency? In essence, mastering your profit and loss is about taking control. It empowers you to make informed choices, avoid pitfalls, and seize opportunities with confidence. It turns abstract numbers into meaningful stories that reflect your business's strengths, challenges, and potential.

As you deepen your understanding of the profit and loss statement, you begin to see beyond just numbers and you start to see your business with clarity and purpose. And that clarity is the foundation upon which sustainable success is built.

In the life of a small business, cash is king. More than profits or assets, the flow of cash in and out of your business determines your ability to survive and thrive. Even a business that is profitable on paper can quickly find itself in trouble if cash flow is mismanaged. Understanding, monitoring, and controlling cash flow is therefore a critical skill every small business owner must master.

Cash flow refers to the actual movement of money as how cash enters your business and how it leaves. It's the lifeblood that keeps everything functioning: paying suppliers, employees, rent, and other bills. Unlike profit, which is an accounting concept that measures income minus expenses over time, cash flow is about liquidity and having the money on hand when you need it.

One of the most common pitfalls small businesses face is confusing profitability with cash availability. A company can show a profit on its financial statements yet run out of cash if payments from customers are delayed or if expenses come due before income is received. For example, if you sell products on credit, you might have many sales booked but no actual cash to cover immediate expenses. This mismatch is the cause of many business failures and can be avoided by diligent cash flow management.

To manage cash flow effectively, the first step is to understand the timing of your cash inflows and outflows. This means knowing when money is coming in such as sales payments, loans, investments and when money must go out in form of payroll, rent, utilities, loan repayments, and inventory purchases. Creating a cash flow forecast helps you predict cash shortages or surpluses in the weeks or months ahead. This foresight allows you to plan proactively rather than reactively, avoiding the stress and disruption of unexpected cash crunches. Tracking your cash flow regularly whether daily or weekly depending on your business size is crucial. This isn't just about accounting entries but about real money in the bank. Reviewing your cash position frequently allows you to spot trends, identify slow-paying customers, or notice increasing expenses before they become problems.

Another critical aspect is managing your accounts receivable and payable efficiently. Encourage prompt payments from customers by offering incentives for early payment or setting clear terms upfront. Likewise, negotiate favorable payment terms with suppliers to extend your cash outflows when possible. This balancing act can smooth cash flow fluctuations and provide breathing room during tight periods.

Controlling expenses is equally important. While some costs are fixed, others can be managed or delayed without harming operations. Regularly reviewing your expenses helps identify unnecessary or excessive spending that drains cash. Every dollar saved on avoidable costs adds to your cash reserves and stability. When cash flow problems arise, small business owners often face difficult choices such as cutting costs, delaying payments, seeking short-term financing, or accelerating sales. Having a contingency plan for such situations, including access to a line of credit or an emergency fund, can be the difference between weathering a tough period and closing the doors.

Technology can be a helpful ally in managing cash flow. Digital accounting and invoicing tools provide real-time updates, reminders, and analytics that help maintain a clear picture of your cash position. They also reduce errors and administrative overhead, freeing you to focus on the strategic aspects of your business. Importantly, cash flow management isn't a one-time fix but an ongoing discipline. As your business grows or market conditions change, your cash flow patterns will evolve. Regularly revisiting and adjusting your forecasts, payment policies, and expense controls ensures you stay in control rather than being controlled by cash flow surprises.

Mastering cash flow also means understanding the difference between operating cash flow and financing cash flow. Operating cash flow comes from your core business activities such as the cash generated or used by selling products and services. Financing cash flow relates to external funding such as loans, investor money, or repayments. Relying too heavily on financing cash flow to cover operating deficits is unsustainable in the long term and can lead to dangerous debt cycles.

Ultimately, cash flow mastery is about creating predictability and control in an area of business that can often feel uncertain and stressful. It empowers you to make informed decisions whether it's investing in growth, hiring staff, or weathering slow seasons because you understand your real-time financial capacity. By demystifying cash flow and integrating it into your regular business practice, you transform it from a source of anxiety into a tool of strength. With this control, you gain not only financial stability but also the confidence to pursue opportunities and handle challenges without fear.

For a small business owner, budgeting often feels like an administrative burden such as a chore to complete rather than a strategic tool. Yet, a purposeful budget is one of the most powerful instruments at your disposal. It transforms guesswork into clarity, turning hopes and ambitions into concrete plans. More than just numbers on a spreadsheet, a budget is a roadmap that guides your business toward stability and sustainable growth.

Budgeting is about allocation: deciding where your money should go, how much should be set aside, and when expenses will occur. Without a budget, a business operates on hope and reaction, hoping there will be enough cash when bills are due, reacting to expenses as they arise, and often scrambling to cover unexpected costs. This approach is a recipe for stress and missed opportunities.

A well-crafted budget begins with understanding your income and expenses in detail. This means digging into your historical financial data to see patterns and trends. Which months bring in the most revenue? Are there seasonal fluctuations? Which expenses are fixed and which vary? This analysis provides the foundation for making realistic assumptions about future financial performance. But budgeting isn't just about predicting the future; it's about setting goals and priorities. What are your business objectives for the coming months or year? Do you plan to hire new staff, launch a marketing campaign, or invest in new equipment? Each goal carries a financial implication, and your budget must reflect these priorities. By aligning your budget with your strategic plans, you ensure that money flows to the areas that drive your vision forward.

Creating a budget also helps identify potential shortfalls before they become crises. By forecasting cash inflows and outflows, you can spot months where expenses might exceed income and plan accordingly. This foresight enables you to arrange financing, delay non-essential spending, or increase sales efforts ahead of time. In this way, budgeting shifts your business from reactive to proactive management.

An effective budget is also flexible. It's a living document that should be revisited regularly such as monthly or quarterly to compare actual results against projections. This review process highlights variances and encourages reflection: Why did revenue fall short? Did an expense exceed expectations? Such questions drive continuous improvement and accountability.

Moreover, budgeting cultivates discipline. It sets spending limits and creates a framework for decision-making. When faced with choices such as should I invest in new software, or save that money? Your budget serves as a reference point. It helps you weigh options in light of financial realities rather than emotions or impulse. Importantly, budgeting supports communication and transparency. Sharing your budget with partners, employees, or investors fosters a culture of trust and shared responsibility. When everyone understands the financial plan, collaboration improves and the entire team works toward common goals.

Another advantage of budgeting is its role in building financial resilience. By anticipating expenses and saving for contingencies, you create a cushion against unexpected challenges. Whether it's a sudden drop in sales, an equipment repair, or a health crisis, a well-funded buffer reduces stress and keeps operations stable. Small business owners often worry about the time and complexity involved in budgeting. However, tools and software have made the process more accessible than ever. Simple spreadsheets or cloud-based platforms can automate calculations, generate reports, and provide visual dashboards. This technology allows you to focus less on the mechanics and more on the insights your budget reveals.

It is a practice of intentionality. It forces you to think critically about how you allocate resources and what success looks like financially. It transforms financial management from a reactive scramble into a strategic advantage. In essence, budgeting with purpose is about empowering your business to navigate uncertainty with confidence.

It provides a clear financial path, aligns spending with goals, and cultivates habits that underpin sustainable growth. For any small business owner, mastering budgeting is not just advisable but it is essential.

Setting the right price for your products or services is both an art and a science and for small business owners, it can be one of the most daunting decisions. Price too low, and you risk eroding your profit margins, devaluing your brand, or failing to sustain your business. Price too high, and you might scare away customers or lose your competitive edge. The challenge is finding the sweet spot where price reflects true value while supporting a healthy profit.

Many entrepreneurs struggle with pricing because it touches on more than just covering costs. It involves understanding your market, your customer's perception, your business goals, and your long-term sustainability. Pricing is not static; it evolves with your business and the changing landscape around you.

The most basic pricing method is cost-plus pricing which is calculating all the costs involved in producing your product or service and adding a markup to ensure profit. While straightforward and essential, relying solely on cost-plus can be limiting. It may not capture the full value your customers perceive or allow you to adjust to market dynamics.

Alternatively, value-based pricing centers on the benefits and unique qualities your offering provides to customers. This approach requires deep insight into customer needs, preferences, and willingness to pay. It emphasizes the outcome or transformation your product enables rather than just the inputs it requires. Businesses that master value-based pricing often command premium prices and build stronger brand loyalty.

To choose the right pricing strategy, you must consider your target market. Are you serving budget-conscious customers, or is your product positioned as a premium offering? Understanding your audience's expectations and price sensitivity is crucial. Conducting market research, analyzing competitors, and gathering direct customer feedback can inform these decisions. Pricing also needs to reflect your business objectives. Are you aiming to quickly gain market share? Then a lower introductory price might make sense. Are you focusing on maximizing profitability? Then a higher price aligned with the value delivered could be better. Pricing should support your overall vision and growth plans.

Don't overlook the psychological aspects of pricing. Pricing endings, perceived value, and even the way prices are presented can influence buying decisions. For example, prices ending in .99 often appear more attractive than rounded numbers. Bundling products or services can also increase perceived value and sales.

Regularly reviewing and adjusting prices is another important practice. Inflation, changing costs, competitor actions, and shifts in customer demand all impact your pricing landscape. Avoid the temptation to keep prices static out of habit. Instead, treat pricing as a dynamic element of your business strategy. Transparency with customers about pricing can build trust, especially if your price changes reflect improvements in quality, service, or value. Clear communication helps customers understand the rationale behind pricing decisions and reduces resistance.

Equally important is knowing when and how to offer discounts or promotions without undermining your pricing integrity. Discounting can be an effective tool for driving sales or clearing inventory but should be used strategically to avoid training customers to expect lower prices. Pricing for profit requires a balance of financial knowledge, market insight, and confidence in the value you provide. It's a continuous learning process, informed by data, customer feedback, and business experience. By valuing your work appropriately and setting prices that reflect both costs and customer perceptions, you create a foundation for sustainable profitability. Pricing well is not just about numbers but it's about honoring your business, your customers, and the future you're building.

One of the most critical yet often overlooked financial practices for small business owners is the clear separation of personal and business finances. At first glance, it might seem convenient or even necessary to mix funds, especially in the early stages of a business when resources are tight. However, this blending can quickly lead to confusion, risk, and serious complications that threaten both your business and personal financial wellbeing.

Separating finances isn't just about organization; it's about protecting yourself legally, financially, and operationally. When business and personal money intermingle, it becomes difficult to track true business performance, making financial management and tax preparation complicated and error-prone. More importantly, this mix can expose your personal assets to business liabilities, increasing your risk in the event of lawsuits, debts, or audits. The foundation of separation starts with establishing a dedicated business bank account. This account serves as the central hub for all business income and expenses. By routing all transactions through this account, you create a clear record of business activity that simplifies accounting and provides an accurate financial picture. It also builds credibility with banks, suppliers, and customers, signaling professionalism and seriousness.

Using a separate business credit card can further aid in managing expenses and building business credit. This tool, when used wisely, can offer benefits like rewards, fraud protection, and streamlined expense tracking. However, caution is necessary to avoid overextending credit or blurring lines between personal spending and business needs. Another key step is setting a clear salary or owner's draw. Rather than sporadically withdrawing money as needed, determine a fixed amount to pay yourself regularly. This practice creates budgeting discipline and helps maintain cash flow stability. It also provides clarity during tax time, as income and expenses are clearly delineated. Keeping accurate and detailed records of all financial transactions supports this separation. Whether through accounting software or manual bookkeeping, careful record-keeping is essential for monitoring business health, preparing financial statements, and complying with tax regulations.

Beyond operational benefits, separating finances can ease tax obligations. Business expenses can be properly deducted, and income accurately reported, reducing the risk of costly mistakes or audits. Many tax authorities scrutinize commingled finances, and failure to maintain separation can trigger penalties. The separation also aids in decision-making. When you see your business finances clearly, free from personal transactions, you can evaluate performance honestly, identify opportunities, and address challenges without distortion. This clarity fosters better planning and strategic thinking. It's important to recognize that financial separation is not a one-time setup but an ongoing commitment. As your business grows, maintain discipline in managing accounts, tracking expenses, and reviewing financial reports. Regularly reconciling your business bank account ensures accuracy and reveals discrepancies early.

For some entrepreneurs, especially sole proprietors, the line between personal and business can feel blurry. However, even informal businesses benefit greatly from clear financial boundaries. As your business evolves, formal structures like LLCs or corporations further reinforce this separation and provide additional legal protections. Drawing a firm line between personal and business finances is a safeguard that preserves your business's integrity, simplifies management, and protects your personal assets. It is a foundational habit that underpins sound financial practices and long-term success.

CHAPTER SIX
REGULATORY READINESS

For every small business owner, the journey begins not only with passion and ideas but also with a responsibility to navigate a complex legal landscape. Compliance which is the act of adhering to laws, regulations, and standards may often seem like an obstacle or a bureaucratic headache, but it is, in truth, one of the most critical pillars supporting the longevity and legitimacy of your business.

At its core, compliance protects your business from legal risks and penalties that can disrupt operations or even lead to closure. Failure to comply with regulations can result in fines, lawsuits, revoked licenses, and damage to your reputation. These consequences can be devastating, especially for small businesses where resources and margins are tight. Understanding the importance of compliance is, therefore, a foundational step toward building a resilient enterprise.

The regulatory environment encompasses a broad spectrum of laws ranging from tax codes and labor laws to environmental regulations and consumer protection statutes. While the specific rules that apply will vary based on your industry, location, and business model, the principle remains the same: respecting the law is non-negotiable. Compliance also instills confidence in your customers, suppliers, and partners. Operating within the bounds of the law signals professionalism and reliability, fostering trust and opening doors to opportunities that might otherwise be closed. In a marketplace crowded with competitors, adherence to legal standards can become a key differentiator.

For many small business owners, the regulatory world can seem intimidating due to its complexity and constant evolution. Laws change, new rules emerge, and what was compliant yesterday may no longer be today. This dynamic nature requires vigilance and a proactive approach to ensure your business stays on the right side of the law. Being compliant does not mean your business must be slowed down by endless paperwork or legal jargon. Instead, it's about integrating regulatory requirements into your daily operations in a way that supports efficiency and growth. It's about creating systems and habits that allow you to meet obligations without losing sight of your core mission.

One important mindset shift is to view compliance not as a cost but as an investment. The resources spent on understanding and following regulations are a small price compared to the financial and reputational damage of non-compliance. Furthermore, compliance can help you avoid unexpected disruptions, allowing you to focus on innovation and serving your customers.

It can open doors to funding, partnerships, and market access. Many lenders and investors require proof of regulatory adherence before committing funds. Similarly, certain contracts or client relationships may hinge on your ability to demonstrate compliance with relevant standards.

The path to compliance begins with knowledge. It requires understanding which laws apply to your business and what specific actions are needed to fulfill those requirements. This process often involves research, consultation with professionals, and continuous learning. Technology can aid greatly in managing compliance. From automated tax filing systems to digital recordkeeping and alert services for regulatory changes, tools exist to simplify the complexity. Leveraging these resources helps you stay organized and reduces the risk of human error.

Finally, compliance is not a one-time achievement but an ongoing commitment. It requires regular review, updates, and adjustments as your business evolves and as laws change. Building a culture that values compliance among yourself and any employees ensures that it becomes part of your business DNA rather than an afterthought. Understanding and embracing compliance is essential for every small business owner who seeks to build a sustainable, trustworthy, and thriving enterprise. Far from a burden, it is a safeguard and a strategic advantage that paves the way for long-term success.

Starting a small business is an exciting venture filled with possibilities, but before you open your doors or launch your website, there's a crucial step you cannot overlook: making your business official through registration and licensing. This foundational process is more than paperwork as it's your first move toward legitimacy, legal protection, and operational readiness.

Business registration establishes your company as a recognized legal entity. Whether you choose to operate as a sole proprietorship, partnership, limited liability company (LLC), or corporation, this decision shapes how your business is viewed by the government, your customers, and potential partners. Registration grants you the rights and responsibilities of doing business within your jurisdiction, including the ability to enter contracts, hire employees, and open business bank accounts.

Choosing the appropriate legal structure is a key part of registration. Each structure has unique implications for liability, taxation, and regulatory compliance. For instance, sole proprietorships are the simplest and cheapest to form but offer no personal liability protection. LLCs and corporations, while more complex and costly to establish, shield your personal assets from business debts and legal claims. Understanding these differences and aligning your choice with your business goals is essential for long-term success. In addition to registering your business name and legal structure, you'll need to obtain the proper licenses and permits. These requirements vary widely depending on your industry, location, and the nature of your operations. Common licenses include sales tax permits, health permits for food businesses, professional licenses for certain trades, and zoning permits for physical locations.

Securing these licenses is not just a regulatory hoop to jump through as it ensures your business complies with safety, health, and operational standards designed to protect consumers and communities. Operating without the necessary licenses can result in fines, shutdowns, or legal action, all of which can be devastating for a small enterprise.

The process of registration and licensing often involves multiple government agencies at local, state, and federal levels. While this may seem daunting, numerous resources are available to guide you. Many jurisdictions offer small business development centers, online portals, and business counselors to assist you through the steps.

Timeliness is critical. Registering and licensing your business before you start operations helps you avoid penalties and positions you to build trust with customers and suppliers. It also allows you to take advantage of business benefits such as tax deductions and eligibility for grants or loans that require proof of legitimacy. Importantly, business registration and licensing are not static milestones but ongoing responsibilities. Licenses may require periodic renewal, and changes in your business model might necessitate additional permits or modifications. Staying on top of these requirements prevents surprises and interruptions. While the initial registration and licensing process requires time and effort, it is a valuable investment in your business's foundation. It protects your interests, ensures legal compliance, and signals to the marketplace that you are a serious and trustworthy player.

Getting legit from day one through proper registration and licensing is a crucial step that turns your entrepreneurial dreams into a credible and sustainable reality. By taking care of these legal essentials early, you create a smoother path for growth, opportunity, and peace of mind.

Taxes are among the most challenging and often intimidating responsibilities small business owners face. The thought of navigating tax codes, deadlines, and payments can feel overwhelming, especially for those without a background in finance or accounting. However, understanding and managing your tax obligations with confidence is crucial as it is not only to avoid costly penalties but also to maximize your business's financial health and sustainability. Taxes are the price businesses pay to operate within a regulated society, funding public services and infrastructure. While taxes may never be popular, they are inevitable. The key is to approach tax responsibilities not as a burdensome chore, but as an integral part of your business strategy.

Small businesses are subject to a variety of taxes depending on their structure, location, and activities. The main categories include income tax, self-employment tax, payroll taxes, sales tax, and sometimes specialized taxes related to specific industries. Understanding these categories and how they apply to your business is the first step toward compliance.

Income tax is the tax you pay on your business profits. How you pay it depends largely on your business's legal structure. For sole proprietors and many partnerships, business income is reported on the owner's personal tax return, a system called pass-through taxation. Corporations, however, file separate tax returns and pay corporate taxes, which adds complexity but can offer advantages under certain circumstances. Self-employment tax is a specific tax that covers Social Security and Medicare contributions for those who work for themselves. If you're a sole proprietor or partner, you'll pay this tax in addition to income tax, reflecting both the employer and employee portions of these contributions. Payroll taxes come into play if you hire employees. These taxes include Social Security, Medicare, federal and state unemployment taxes, and income tax withholding. Employers have a legal obligation to collect, report, and remit these taxes accurately and timely.

Sales tax applies if your business sells tangible goods or certain services. The rules around sales tax can be complex, varying by state, county, and city. Some jurisdictions require businesses to collect and remit sales tax, while others do not. Understanding where you have a sales tax nexus meaning a significant presence that obligates you to collect tax is essential. Other specialized taxes might include excise taxes on certain goods like fuel, tobacco, or alcohol, or industry-specific levies. While not common for all small businesses, knowing if your industry has such requirements is important to avoid surprises.

Accurate and organized recordkeeping is the backbone of effective tax management. Good records help you track income and expenses, support deductions, and prepare reliable financial statements. They also make tax filing less stressful and provide a clear paper trail in case of an audit. Your records should include all sales receipts, invoices, bank statements, canceled checks, payroll documents, and any correspondence with tax authorities. Using digital tools or accounting software can streamline this process, offering automatic categorization and report generation. Maintaining separate accounts for business and personal finances simplifies recordkeeping and reduces errors. It also ensures transparency and credibility with tax authorities.

One of the benefits of being a small business owner is access to a variety of tax deductions and credits that can significantly reduce your taxable income. Deductions reduce the amount of income subject to tax, while credits directly reduce the tax owed.

Common deductions include business expenses like rent, utilities, office supplies, travel, marketing, insurance, and salaries. Capital expenses for equipment and property may also be deductible, sometimes immediately or through depreciation over time. Tax credits are often more specific and targeted. Examples include credits for hiring veterans or employees from certain groups, investing in renewable energy, or research and development activities. Understanding which deductions and credits apply to your business and keeping thorough documentation is essential to maximize these benefits.

Missing deadlines or underpaying taxes can trigger penalties and interest charges that drain resources and distract from your business goals. Establishing a tax calendar that includes all relevant due dates for estimated tax payments, payroll tax filings, and annual returns is vital. Many small businesses pay taxes quarterly, particularly for income and self-employment taxes. Payroll taxes are typically reported and paid monthly or quarterly, depending on your payroll size. Sales taxes may require monthly or quarterly remittance as well. Using automated reminders, calendar alerts, or working with an accountant can help you stay on track. Timely payment avoids penalties and ensures your business maintains good standing with tax authorities.

While many small business owners handle taxes themselves, engaging a qualified accountant or tax professional can be a wise investment. Professionals bring expertise that helps optimize your tax position, avoid errors, and navigate complex issues.

Accountants can assist with tax planning by structuring your business activities and finances to minimize taxes legally. They also provide peace of mind by preparing and reviewing your tax returns and representing you in case of audits. Though audits are rare for small businesses, they do happen. Having clean, organized records and staying truthful and consistent in your filings is the best defense. If audited, cooperation and professional guidance can make the process less stressful.

The most successful small business owners don't treat taxes as a year-end event but as an ongoing responsibility. They track finances throughout the year, anticipate liabilities, and plan accordingly. Proactive tax management means setting aside funds regularly to cover tax payments, understanding the tax implications of business decisions, and continuously educating yourself on tax changes. By mastering your tax obligations and adopting a proactive approach, you transform tax season from a source of stress into a strategic opportunity for your business. Confidence in tax management empowers you to focus on growth while staying firmly compliant.

As your small business grows, the prospect of hiring employees brings both exciting opportunities and new responsibilities. Employment law, often seen as a complex and intimidating field, is essential knowledge for every small business owner who seeks to build a fair, safe, and legally compliant workplace. Understanding the basics not only protects your business from costly disputes and penalties but also fosters a positive environment that attracts and retains talented staff. Employment laws cover a broad range of areas, from hiring practices and employee classification to wages, benefits, workplace safety, and termination procedures. While laws vary by country and even by state or locality, certain fundamental principles apply universally and form the foundation for good employment management.

One of the first areas to understand is the distinction between employees and independent contractors. Misclassifying workers can lead to significant legal and financial consequences, including back taxes, penalties, and lawsuits. Employees generally receive more protections under labor laws, including minimum wage guarantees, overtime pay, and benefits, while contractors operate as self-employed individuals with more control over how they complete work.

Hiring practices must comply with anti-discrimination laws that prohibit unfair treatment based on race, gender, age, religion, disability, or other protected characteristics. These laws ensure that every candidate receives equal consideration and that your hiring decisions are based on merit and fit rather than bias or prejudice. Once hired, employees are entitled to fair wages and hours, which often include adherence to minimum wage laws and overtime regulations. Keeping accurate payroll records is not only a legal requirement but also critical for building trust and avoiding disputes. Transparent communication about compensation, benefits, and expectations helps set the tone for a positive workplace culture.

Workplace safety is another cornerstone of employment law. Depending on your industry, you may be required to meet specific health and safety standards designed to prevent accidents and protect employees' well-being. Regular training, hazard assessments, and compliance with Occupational Safety and Health Administration (OSHA) guidelines, or their equivalent, are vital practices. Employee benefits, such as health insurance, retirement plans, and leave policies, are increasingly important for attracting and retaining staff. While some benefits are mandated by law, others may be offered voluntarily as part of your company's compensation package. Clear documentation and communication about these benefits reduce misunderstandings and build loyalty. Employment contracts or written agreements clarify the terms of employment, including job responsibilities, compensation, confidentiality, and grounds for termination. These contracts serve as a reference point for both parties and can prevent misunderstandings or legal disputes.

Termination of employment must be handled with care and in accordance with relevant laws. Whether ending a position due to performance issues, restructuring, or mutual agreement, following proper procedures such as including notice requirements and final paycheck rules protects your business from wrongful termination claims. Beyond these basics, staying updated on changes in employment law is crucial. Laws evolve to reflect societal changes, court rulings, and political priorities, meaning what was compliant last year may not be today. Building a relationship with a labor law expert or human resources consultant can provide ongoing guidance.

Importantly, treating employees with respect, fairness, and clear communication fosters a positive workplace culture that extends beyond mere legal compliance. Happy and well-managed employees are more productive, engaged, and loyal are qualities that are especially valuable for small businesses. In summary, understanding and applying employment law basics is a critical responsibility that supports not only legal compliance but also the growth and reputation of your small business. By respecting employee rights and meeting your responsibilities, you build a foundation for a healthy, thriving workplace where both your business and your people can succeed.

In the life of a small business owner, one constant remains unchanged: the regulatory environment is always evolving. Laws change, new rules emerge, and compliance requirements shift in response to political, economic, and social developments. Staying current with these changes is not a luxury as it's a necessity for maintaining your business's legal standing and competitive edge. Many small business owners find regulatory updates overwhelming. The sheer volume of information, combined with the technical language and sometimes conflicting advice, can lead to confusion or inaction. However, the consequences of missing or ignoring important regulatory changes are severe. Non-compliance can result in fines, legal action, or even forced closure, and it can damage your reputation among customers and partners.

The good news is that staying up-to-date doesn't require full-time legal expertise or hiring expensive consultants. With the right tools and habits, you can build an efficient system to monitor and adapt to changes without losing focus on your core business operations.

One of the first steps is to identify the key regulatory bodies and resources that govern your business. This often includes local government agencies, state departments, and federal organizations related to taxation, labor, environmental standards, and industry-specific regulations. Bookmarking their official websites and subscribing to newsletters or alerts ensures that important announcements come directly to you.

Technology offers powerful tools for regulatory monitoring. There are software platforms and services specifically designed to track changes in laws and compliance requirements relevant to your business sector. These tools can send notifications, provide summaries, and even offer guidance on implementing changes. Networking with other small business owners in your industry or community is another effective way to stay informed. Business associations, chambers of commerce, and professional groups often share updates, best practices, and interpretations of new regulations. Engaging in these networks creates a support system where you can learn from others' experiences and ask questions.

Developing a regular review routine is essential. Setting aside dedicated time each month or quarter to review regulatory updates, assess your compliance status, and plan necessary adjustments integrates regulatory awareness into your business rhythm. This prevents surprises and allows you to respond proactively. Documentation is key to demonstrating compliance over time. Keeping organized records of how your business meets regulatory requirements, including training records, permits, inspections, and correspondence, provides evidence in case of audits or inquiries. Sometimes, regulatory changes require adjustments in your business practices, policies, or systems. Approaching these changes with flexibility and a problem-solving mindset helps you turn challenges into opportunities. For example, adopting new environmental regulations might inspire innovations that improve efficiency or reduce costs.

When faced with complex or ambiguous regulatory changes, don't hesitate to seek professional advice. Lawyers, accountants, and consultants specializing in compliance can clarify your obligations and recommend appropriate actions, saving you time and reducing risk. Embedding regulatory readiness into your business culture is the most sustainable approach. Educating yourself and your employees about compliance expectations fosters vigilance and shared responsibility. When everyone understands the importance of staying current, your business is better equipped to adapt and thrive.

Regulatory changes are an unavoidable part of running a small business, but they need not be a source of stress or confusion. By using the right tools, cultivating habits of regular review, and building networks of support, you can stay ahead of the curve and ensure your business remains compliant, competitive, and ready for whatever the future holds.

CHAPTER SEVEN
PEOPLE AND PRODUCTIVITY

Hiring the right people is one of the most important decisions a small business owner can make. For a small-scale enterprise, every team member matters profoundly. Unlike large corporations with vast resources and extensive HR departments, small businesses often operate with limited budgets, fewer personnel, and less brand recognition. These challenges can make recruitment seem daunting, yet hiring thoughtfully and strategically can propel a business from survival to thriving.

Recruitment for small businesses is about finding individuals whose skills, values, and ambitions align closely with the company's vision and needs. Unlike mass hiring or filling a vast number of roles, the process here is deeply personal and nuanced. Each hire has the potential to impact the company culture, customer experience, and operational efficiency.

One of the first considerations is defining what "the right fit" means for your business. This goes beyond qualifications or past experience. It includes attitude, adaptability, willingness to learn, and cultural compatibility. In a small team, personalities and interpersonal dynamics become magnified. An employee who embraces the company's mission and works well with others can drive team cohesion and productivity. The hiring process begins well before interviews. Crafting a clear, compelling job description is essential. This document should not only list required skills and responsibilities but also convey the company's unique identity and the role's potential impact. Job descriptions tailored to small businesses often emphasize versatility and entrepreneurial spirit, signaling to candidates that flexibility and initiative are valued.

Where to find candidates is another critical question. Small businesses may not attract the volume of applicants that larger firms do, but they can leverage targeted and creative strategies. Local networks, community boards, industry groups, and social media platforms are invaluable resources. Employee referrals, often overlooked, can yield candidates who are pre-vetted and culturally aligned.

Once applications come in, the screening process must be rigorous but efficient. Reviewing resumes carefully, looking for indicators of both technical skill and soft skills, sets the stage for meaningful interviews. For small businesses, interviews are an opportunity to assess not only experience but character and potential. Structured questions that explore problem-solving, teamwork, and past challenges can reveal how candidates might behave in your unique environment. The interview itself should be a two-way conversation.

Candidates today seek authenticity and want to understand the company's culture, expectations, and growth opportunities. Sharing stories about your business journey, challenges, and values invites candidates to envision themselves within your organization.

Beyond traditional interviews, practical assessments or trial projects can provide practical insights into a candidate's capabilities. While these require time investment, they reduce the risk of hiring mismatches and set clear expectations.

Onboarding is a critical phase that often gets underestimated in small businesses. A thoughtful onboarding process eases new hires into their roles, familiarizes them with company practices, and fosters early engagement. It sets the tone for their experience and can influence retention significantly. Even simple gestures, like assigning a mentor or providing clear documentation, make a difference.

Small businesses must also be mindful of legal compliance during hiring. This includes proper documentation, adherence to labor laws, and nondiscriminatory practices. While administrative, these steps protect the business and reinforce professional standards. Retention begins at hiring but extends into ongoing employee relations. Small businesses, limited in resources, can't always compete on salary with larger firms. Instead, they often succeed by offering meaningful work, flexible arrangements, and a sense of ownership. Communicating openly, recognizing contributions, and fostering growth opportunities help keep talent motivated.

In many ways, recruitment in small businesses is an art as it involves balancing intuition with process, judgment with data, and pragmatism with aspiration. It demands patience, openness, and a willingness to invest time and energy. But the payoff is enormous. Building a team that truly fits the business's needs and culture creates a foundation for success that no amount of capital can easily replace. In the end, the right hire is someone who not only fills a job description but also embraces your vision and commits to growing alongside your business. Approaching recruitment with this mindset turns hiring into a strategic advantage, one that fuels productivity, innovation, and long-term resilience.

In the early stages of a small business, team members often wear many hats, fluidly shifting between tasks as needs arise. This flexibility can be strength such as allowing quick adaptation, personal growth, and shared understanding of the business. However, as the business grows and the team expands, this informal approach can start to undermine efficiency, create confusion, and breed frustration. It is here that clearly defining roles and responsibilities becomes not just beneficial but essential.

Defining roles means setting clear expectations about who is responsible for what. It involves specifying duties, decision-making authority, accountability, and the relationships between different positions. While this may sound like corporate bureaucracy better suited to large companies, the reality is quite different. For small businesses, where resources are tight and every action counts, clarity in roles can streamline operations, reduce overlap, and empower employees to work confidently and independently.

When roles are vague or overlapping, several problems commonly arise. Employees may duplicate efforts unknowingly, wasting time and resources. Critical tasks may fall through the cracks because everyone assumed someone else was handling them. Conflicts can emerge over authority or turf, distracting from the work itself. Without clarity, measuring performance and providing feedback also becomes difficult, since it's unclear what success looks like for each role.

The starting point for defining roles is understanding your business's core functions. Every small business has essential activities that drive its operations and growth, be it sales, customer service, product development, marketing, finance, or administration. Mapping these out provides a framework for allocating responsibilities.

Once core functions are identified, the next step is creating job descriptions that articulate the purpose and scope of each role. These should detail key tasks, expected outcomes, necessary skills, and reporting lines. Writing these descriptions with input from current employees can ensure accuracy and buy-in. It also allows employees to see how their work fits into the broader picture, increasing engagement. An effective role definition balances specificity with flexibility. Too rigid a description risks stifling creativity and responsiveness; too vague leaves room for misunderstanding. For small businesses, it's often wise to include a degree of role fluidity by acknowledging that employees may occasionally step outside strict boundaries when business demands shift.

Clear responsibilities also empower decision-making. When employees understand the limits and extent of their authority, they can act without constant supervision or second-guessing. This autonomy not only speeds up processes but fosters ownership and accountability, key drivers of productivity in small teams. Equally important is clarifying how roles interact. Defining communication channels, collaboration points, and escalation paths reduces friction and ensures smooth workflow. Regular team meetings or check-ins provide opportunities to revisit roles and resolve any overlaps or gaps.

In practice, many small business owners initially take on multiple roles themselves. While this is natural and often necessary in the early phase, it's crucial to recognize when to delegate. Holding on to too many responsibilities can bottleneck progress and lead to burnout. Delegation requires trust and clear role definitions so that tasks handed off are executed effectively.

For new hires, role clarity is foundational to successful onboarding. When new employees receive well-defined expectations from day one, they can focus on delivering value rather than guessing their duties. Clear roles also facilitate targeted training, helping employees develop the specific skills they need. Performance management is tightly linked to roles and responsibilities. Without defined criteria for success, appraisals become subjective and ineffective. Clear roles enable objective assessment based on measurable outcomes, which in turn guides coaching and development.

Small businesses often rely on cross-functional collaboration, especially when teams are small. While this encourages learning and flexibility, it also heightens the need for role clarity. Knowing who leads what aspect of a project, who provides support, and who is accountable for results keeps teamwork efficient and focused. Technology can assist in defining and communicating roles. Tools like shared project management software, organizational charts, and responsibility matrices provide visual clarity and reference points. Digital documentation accessible to the whole team reduces ambiguity and ensures everyone is aligned.

As your business evolves, roles will naturally shift. Regularly reviewing and updating role definitions ensures they remain relevant and effective. Engaging employees in this process encourages ownership and adaptability.

Defining roles and responsibilities is about respect which includes respect for your team's time, talents, and efforts. It creates an environment where everyone knows what to expect from themselves and others, minimizing confusion and maximizing impact. By establishing clarity, small businesses lay the groundwork for efficiency, accountability, and growth. It transforms the chaos of overlapping duties into a well-orchestrated operation where every person contributes to shared goals with confidence and purpose.

In the intimate environment of a small business, culture isn't just a buzzword as it's the heartbeat that drives everything. Unlike large corporations where culture can become diffuse or abstract, in a small team, culture is lived and felt in every interaction, decision, and process. It shapes how employees relate to their work, to each other, and to the business itself. Building a positive culture is not just about perks or slogans; it's about creating a shared sense of purpose, trust, and belonging that amplifies motivation and productivity.

The power of culture in a small business cannot be overstated. When team members feel connected to a meaningful mission and to one another, they bring energy, creativity, and loyalty that far exceed what salary alone can inspire. This emotional investment translates into better customer service, higher quality work, and a collaborative spirit that can weather challenges.

However, building such a culture requires intentionality. It doesn't happen by accident or simply by hiring "good people." It is the product of consistent actions, clear values, and leadership that models the behaviors it wants to see. At its core, culture starts with purpose. A small business often arises from a founder's vision or passion whether it's crafting artisan products, providing excellent service, or solving a unique problem. Communicating this purpose regularly reminds the team why their work matters beyond just the bottom line. It helps align efforts and inspires commitment.

Transparency is another pillar of positive culture. In small teams, openness about company goals, challenges, and decisions fosters trust and inclusion. Employees who understand the business context feel more empowered to contribute ideas and take ownership. Conversely, secrecy or inconsistent messaging breeds suspicion and disengagement.

Respectful communication lays the groundwork for psychological safety as the feeling that individuals can speak up, share concerns, or take risks without fear of ridicule or retaliation. This safety is critical for innovation and problem-solving, especially in small businesses where adaptability is key. Leaders can cultivate this by listening actively, encouraging dialogue, and responding constructively to feedback. Recognition and appreciation fuel motivation in profound ways. Small gestures such as a sincere thank-you, public acknowledgment of effort, or celebrating milestones create positive reinforcement loops that energize the team. In a small business, where formal reward systems may be limited, these personal touches are vital.

Another element of culture is work-life balance and flexibility. Small businesses often pride themselves on agility, which can translate into accommodating personal needs and schedules. This flexibility not only supports employee well-being but can increase loyalty and reduce turnover.

Creating opportunities for learning and growth also contributes to a vibrant culture. When employees see a path for development, they invest more deeply in their roles. This might mean cross-training, access to courses, or simply encouraging curiosity and experimentation.

The physical workspace, even if modest, influences culture as well. A welcoming, organized, and comfortable environment signals that people and their experience matter. Whether it's a shared lunch area, personalized workstations, or simple team rituals, these details build connection and identity. Culture is shaped daily through leadership behavior. Small business leaders set the tone by how they treat people, manage stress, and respond to setbacks. Authenticity and humility build respect, while inconsistency undermines it. Leading by example means demonstrating the values the business espouses. Conflict is inevitable in any team, but culture determines how it is handled. A positive culture encourages addressing issues promptly and respectfully, focusing on solutions rather than blame. This approach preserves relationships and strengthens collaboration.

Small businesses benefit from involving employees in culture-building. Soliciting input on policies, traditions, or social activities increases engagement and ownership. This inclusion signals that everyone's voice matters. Ultimately, culture is a strategic asset for small businesses. It differentiates the business in competitive markets, attracting customers and talent who resonate with its ethos. Positive culture enhances resilience, enabling the team to navigate uncertainty and change more effectively.

While it takes effort and attention, building a strong culture doesn't require large budgets or complex programs. It thrives on authenticity, consistent values, and genuine care. Every small business has the power to cultivate a culture where people feel valued, inspired, and connected and that is a culture that transforms a small team into a powerhouse of productivity and impact.

For a small business, managing performance is both an art and a necessity. Without formalized structures or large HR teams, many small business owners face the challenge of keeping their team motivated, productive, and aligned toward shared goals. Yet, effective performance management isn't about complex systems or rigid processes but it's about clear communication, consistent support, and fostering growth.

At its essence, performance management involves setting clear expectations, monitoring progress, and providing constructive feedback that helps employees improve and thrive. It connects individual effort to broader business objectives, ensuring that everyone pulls in the same direction. For small businesses, this process starts with goal setting. Unlike large corporations with sprawling objectives, small businesses benefit from focused, specific, and achievable goals that relate directly to the company's current priorities. Setting clear goals clarifies what success looks like and guides day-to-day actions.

Good goal-setting follows principles that make objectives meaningful and measurable. The popular SMART framework which stands for Specific, Measurable, Achievable, Relevant, and Time-bound can be adapted to the scale of small businesses. For example, a sales associate might have a goal to increase customer follow-ups by 20% over the next quarter, which is concrete and trackable.

Collaborative goal-setting strengthens commitment. When employees participate in defining their own goals, they feel greater ownership and motivation. This also allows managers to align individual aspirations with business needs, creating a win-win scenario. Once goals are in place, tracking progress becomes essential. In small teams, this often happens through informal check-ins rather than formal reviews. Regular conversations provide opportunities to celebrate achievements, identify obstacles, and recalibrate efforts as needed.

Feedback is the lifeblood of performance management. Delivering feedback effectively requires both timing and tone. Immediate feedback, when appropriate, helps correct course quickly. Scheduled sessions allow deeper reflection on performance trends and development areas. Constructive feedback focuses on behaviors and outcomes rather than personalities. It's specific, balanced, and aimed at helping employees grow rather than criticize. For example, instead of saying "You're not doing well," a more helpful approach is "I noticed some missed deadlines last month, let's talk about what might be causing that and how I can support you."

Listening is as important as speaking during feedback. Encouraging employees to share their perspectives uncovers underlying issues, builds trust, and fosters collaboration on solutions. Small business owners can also use positive feedback to reinforce good performance. Recognizing efforts publicly or privately boosts morale and encourages continued excellence. Performance management is not solely about correction; it's about development. Identifying strengths and areas for improvement informs training and coaching opportunities. Small businesses often lack formal training budgets, but creative approaches like peer learning, online courses, or mentoring can be effective.

Setting performance expectations extends beyond individual employees to team dynamics. Clear communication about how roles interconnect and how collaboration contributes to goals reduces friction and enhances efficiency. Documentation of performance discussions, goals, and outcomes provides a reference for future reviews and supports fairness and transparency. Finally, performance management must be flexible and adaptive. Small businesses face rapidly changing environments and priorities. Regularly revisiting goals and feedback ensures that performance management remains relevant and responsive.

When done well, performance management transforms the workplace into a space where employees feel valued, guided, and challenged. It fosters a culture of continuous improvement and accountability without the need for complex bureaucracy. In the hands of small business leaders, effective performance management becomes a powerful tool to unlock individual potential, strengthen teams, and drive sustainable growth.

In small businesses, leadership often looks very different than in large corporations. Without vast hierarchies or formal titles, small business leaders wield influence more than authority. This distinction matters profoundly. Leadership by influence means inspiring, guiding, and motivating your team through respect, trust, and example rather than relying on positional power or rigid commands.

Small-scale business leadership is uniquely challenging yet deeply rewarding. Leaders are typically involved in every aspect of the business from sales and operations to customer service and finance. This breadth of responsibility demands a leadership style that is adaptable, empathetic, and collaborative.

The first and most crucial element of leadership in a small business is authenticity. Employees recognize and respond to genuine leaders who are transparent about their vision, values, and challenges. Authentic leaders admit mistakes, share successes, and communicate openly. This honesty builds trust which is the foundation of influence. Influence grows through relationships. Small business leaders have the advantage of working closely with their teams, creating personal connections that large corporations often lack. Taking time to understand employees' motivations, strengths, and concerns helps leaders tailor their approach and create an environment where people feel valued and supported.

Effective communication is another cornerstone of leadership. This goes beyond simply sharing information. It involves active listening, empathy, and clarity. Leaders must be able to articulate the business's goals and the role each team member plays in achieving them. Equally important is encouraging feedback and fostering two-way dialogue that empowers employees to contribute ideas and raise concerns. Leaders also set the tone for the workplace culture through their behavior. Showing respect, maintaining composure during stress, and demonstrating a strong work ethic models the standards expected throughout the team. Small actions such as acknowledging effort, celebrating small wins, or offering encouragement can have outsized effects.

Decision-making is a daily leadership function that requires balance. Small business leaders often operate with limited information and high uncertainty. Exercising sound judgment means weighing risks, seeking input from the team when appropriate, and being willing to make tough calls. Leaders who involve their team in decisions where possible enhance buy-in and collective responsibility.

Empowerment is central to leadership by influence. This means providing employees with the tools, resources, and authority to perform their jobs effectively and make decisions within their scope. Empowered employees feel trusted and motivated, which drives engagement and productivity. Conflict resolution is another leadership skill that must be handled delicately in small teams. Addressing disputes promptly and fairly preserves relationships and maintains morale. Leaders who approach conflicts with empathy and a problem-solving mindset turn challenges into opportunities for growth.

Mentoring and coaching are vital leadership roles in small businesses. Leaders who invest time in developing their team's skills and confidence cultivate loyalty and build bench strength for the future. This nurturing approach creates a pipeline of talent ready to take on greater responsibilities as the business grows.

Small business leaders also face the ongoing challenge of balancing hands-on involvement with delegation. Micromanagement stifles initiative and can overwhelm leaders, while too much distance can leave teams unsupported. Finding the right balance involves trusting employees while remaining accessible for guidance. Self-awareness is a hallmark of effective leadership. Leaders who understand their strengths and weaknesses seek feedback, continuously learn, and adapt their style. This humility fosters respect and creates a culture of continuous improvement. In small businesses, leadership extends beyond the internal team. Leaders must also cultivate relationships with customers, suppliers, and community partners. Representing the business with integrity and professionalism strengthens reputation and opens doors for growth.

Leading with influence is about inspiring others to follow because they want to, not because they have to. It's a leadership style built on connection, trust, and shared purpose. For small business owners, mastering this approach turns daily challenges into opportunities and transforms a group of individuals into a cohesive, motivated team. This leadership philosophy does not rely on formal power or hierarchy but on the leader's ability to engage hearts and minds. It creates an environment where people feel seen, heard, and motivated to contribute their best.

Small business leaders who lead with influence pave the way for sustainable success. Their leadership resonates far beyond the workplace, shaping the culture, productivity, and ultimately, the legacy of the business.

CHAPTER EIGHT
BRANDING, VISIBLITY AND MARKET POSITIONING

When most people hear the word "brand," their minds jump immediately to visuals such as logos, color schemes, fonts, packaging. But a brand is much more than its aesthetics. Especially for small businesses, where every interaction and impression matters, a brand is the promise you make to your customers and the emotional fingerprint you leave behind. It's not just how your business looks, but how it feels, how it speaks, and how it's remembered. Crafting a clear brand identity is about building a cohesive, authentic presence that tells people who you are, what you stand for, and why they should care.

In the noisy and competitive world of commerce, clarity is power. A clear brand identity gives your business a voice in the crowd. It ensures that your audience knows what you offer, what makes you different, and what they can consistently expect from you. For small businesses, this clarity can be the difference between being remembered and being overlooked.

The foundation of any strong brand identity begins with self-awareness. Before designing a logo or launching a campaign, small business owners need to ask some critical questions: What is the core mission of this business? What values are non-negotiable? Who are we serving, and why do we matter to them? These questions may seem abstract, but the answers shape every outward-facing element of your brand.

Mission and values aren't just nice ideas to stick on a poster. They guide decision-making, messaging, and customer experience. For example, a local café that values sustainability will make different choices from suppliers to packaging than one focused purely on speed and convenience. That sense of mission then becomes part of the brand story that customers connect with emotionally. Equally important is understanding your audience. A brand isn't created in a vacuum as it exists in the minds of those it seeks to serve. What do your customers care about? What language do they use? What kind of visuals catches their eye? What emotions drive their buying decisions? Crafting your brand with your audience in mind ensures that your identity feels relevant and engaging, rather than forced or out of touch.

This is where the visual elements come into play, not as the beginning of branding, but as the embodiment of it. A logo, when done well, becomes a symbol of everything your business stands for. Colors evoke emotion such as blues for trust, reds for energy, greens for growth. Fonts convey tone such as sleek sans-serifs for modern brands, elegant serifs for traditional ones. All these choices should be rooted in intention, not trends. But identity goes far beyond visuals. Your brand has a voice as how you speak to your customers in your marketing materials, on social media, in your emails, and face-to-face. Is your tone friendly and informal? Professional and polished? Playful or serious? Consistency in tone builds familiarity, and familiarity breeds trust.

One of the most powerful parts of brand identity for small businesses is the story. People don't connect with businesses; they connect with stories. Why did you start? What challenge are you trying to solve? What values fuel your journey? Sharing your story, not in a manufactured or overly polished way, but in a sincere and human voice, creates an emotional anchor. It transforms your business from a service provider into a relatable, memorable entity.

Brand identity also extends into the experience your customers have with you from their first visit to your website to how they feel when they unbox your product or leave your store. Is the experience consistent with what your brand promises? A wellness brand, for instance, can't just use soothing colors and fonts; it needs to deliver calm and care in every interaction. A tech brand promising simplicity must make its systems truly intuitive.

In a small business, where personal touch and founder involvement are often front and center, brand identity is deeply personal. Your own values and personality naturally shape how your business shows up in the world. That is strength to be embraced, not hidden. Customers often choose small businesses because they crave connection and authenticity which are things big brands struggle to deliver. When your brand identity reflects your genuine self and beliefs, it resonates more deeply. Of course, as your business evolves, so too may your brand identity. That's normal. The key is to evolve intentionally. Periodically revisiting your brand's core elements ensures they still align with your mission and audience. Businesses that grow without revisiting their brand often find themselves sending mixed signals which is one message on their website, another in-store, and yet another on social media.

Creating a brand guide is a simple document that outlines your mission, tone, visual standards, and key messaging which helps maintain consistency, especially as your team grows. It doesn't need to be long or technical. Even a few pages can provide clarity for anyone creating content or representing your business. A common trap small businesses fall into is mimicking the branding of larger competitors or trendy startups. While it's wise to study what works in the marketplace, blindly copying others dilutes your own identity and erodes trust. Customers can spot inauthenticity, and they gravitate toward brands that feel original and self-assured.

Remember, your brand is also shaped by your community. Customer feedback, reviews, and social engagement all influence how people perceive you. Listening to what your audience is saying, what they praise or criticize, gives you valuable insight into how your brand is actually experienced. This feedback loop is not a threat as it's a gift. It helps you refine your identity in ways that keep it grounded and relevant. Building a strong brand identity is an act of alignment. It's aligning your internal mission and values with your external expression such as your visuals, your words, your customer experience. It's about creating a consistent, memorable presence that reflects who you are and draws the right people toward you.

In the world of small business, where resources are often limited and competition is fierce, your brand is one of your most valuable assets. It tells your story when you're not in the room. It builds trust before a sale is made. It inspires loyalty long after a transaction is complete. And when crafted with care and clarity, it becomes a lighthouse; guiding your business forward and helping your customers find their way to you.

Every successful brand begins not with a product, but with people. The small business owner who truly understands their audience holds the most powerful tool in the entrepreneurial arsenal is relevance. When your brand speaks directly to the values, needs, and emotions of your audience, it doesn't have to shout to be heard. It resonates. And resonance is what builds loyalty, trust, and community. To build visibility that means something, you must first understand who you're trying to reach and why they should care.

Small businesses have an advantage here. They are naturally closer to their customers. They interact with them personally, hear their stories, answer their emails, and see their reactions in real time. This proximity offers invaluable insight, yet too often, business owners rely on assumptions about their audience rather than truly listening. When decisions are based on hunches instead of real, observed behavior, branding and marketing can easily drift off course.

Understanding your audience starts with empathy. It's about putting yourself in their shoes and seeing your business from their perspective. What challenges are they facing? What kind of lifestyle do they lead? What motivates their purchases such as price, convenience, values, status? These are not just marketing questions; they're foundational to how you shape your offerings, communicate your value, and grow sustainably. Demographics such as age, gender, income, education give you the outlines of who your customers are. Psychographics such as values, interests, habits, beliefs fill in the color. But the real understanding comes from behavior. What are your customers actually doing? What are they buying? When do they engage? Where do they drop off?

One of the best tools for this understanding is feedback. Feedback isn't just what people say on a survey but it's every comment, complaint, and compliment. It's in reviews, emails, social media replies, and face-to-face conversations. Feedback is the voice of your audience, and learning to listen to it with curiosity rather than defensiveness is one of the most powerful skills a small business owner can develop. Instead of fearing criticism, lean into it. Negative feedback often reveals areas of confusion, unmet needs, or broken expectations. It gives you a chance to improve not just your product or service, but your relationship with your audience. Thanking someone for pointing out a flaw and then showing you're willing to act on it builds credibility. Customers notice when you listen, and they reward that attention with trust.

Positive feedback, on the other hand, is equally instructive. It shows what's working, what people love about your business and what keeps them coming back. These are your brand strengths, and they should be amplified. When customers use certain words repeatedly to describe your business such as "friendly," "fast," "reliable," "unique", those are clues to how your brand is perceived and where it's already connecting.

Gathering feedback can be formal or informal. Surveys, interviews, and polls are structured methods. But don't underestimate the power of simply talking to your customers by asking questions at the end of a transaction, checking in on their satisfaction, or inviting open comments online. Small businesses have the unique ability to do this in a personal, conversational way that feels natural and sincere.

Understanding your audience also means segmenting them. Not all customers are the same, and trying to speak to everyone often results in connecting with no one. Segmenting your audience allows you to tailor your messaging, products, and experiences. You might have one group of customers who value affordability and another who prioritize sustainability. Recognizing and addressing these segments deepens engagement and drives more meaningful interaction.

Social media and website analytics provide another layer of insight. Tools like Google Analytics, Instagram Insights, or email open rates tell you what content resonate, when people are engaging, and where they're coming from. These aren't just numbers as they're behavioral signals that guide your decisions. But data alone isn't enough. It needs to be interpreted through the lens of real human experience. Numbers tell you what is happening, but you still need to uncover why. Why did sales spike after that post? Why are people spending more time on one page than another? The more you ask "why," the more you uncover about your audience's journey and mindset.

As your audience evolves, your understanding must evolve with it. Trends shift, preferences change, and the way people consume content is always in motion. Staying close to your customers means staying open, open to learning, adapting, and growing with them. Businesses that cling to outdated assumptions about their audience become irrelevant. Those that remain curious and responsive stay vital. The language you use is also shaped by audience understanding. Speaking in the tone, vocabulary, and rhythm that your audience feels comfortable with makes your communication more relatable. This doesn't mean pandering or pretending but it means aligning your message with how your audience already sees the world.

Building a brand that lasts is about forming relationships, not transactions. And no relationship thrives without understanding. Knowing your audience isn't a one-time exercise; it's an ongoing dialogue, a constant process of paying attention and responding with care. When you take the time to truly understand your audience, everything else becomes easier. Your marketing becomes more effective. Your product development becomes more focused. Your messaging becomes clearer. And your business becomes more resilient.

In a crowded marketplace, being seen isn't enough. You have to be seen as relevant. That relevance comes from knowing who you're talking to and why your voice matters to them. Small businesses that get this right don't just sell but they connect, inspire, and endure.

In a marketplace saturated with noise and repetition, storytelling has become the lifeline for small businesses seeking to stand out, not by shouting louder, but by speaking with sincerity. Your story is the soul of your brand. It's what draws people in, holds their attention, and makes them remember you long after they've left your website, your shop, or your inbox. More than any marketing tactic, a well-told story creates emotional connection and in the world of small business, connection is currency.

Telling your story isn't just about your history. It's about expressing the values, motivations, and moments that shape who you are and what you offer. And when done right, storytelling doesn't just describe your brand rather it embodies it. The language you use, the visuals you share, and the rhythm of your content all speak volumes about what you stand for. Every small business has a story. Maybe it's the journey of turning a side hustle into a livelihood. Maybe it's a mission born out of frustration with the status quo. Maybe it's a legacy handed down, reimagined through new eyes. Whatever your origin, your story matters not because it's perfect or dramatic, but because it's real. Authenticity is what cuts through the fluff and fosters trust.

Your story begins with your "why" which is the deeper reason your business exists beyond making money. Simon Sinek popularized this concept in his book *Start with Why*, and it's especially relevant for small businesses. Customers want to know what drives you. Why do you care about this product, this service, this industry? Why did you choose this path over another? When you share your "why," you invite customers to become part of something bigger than a transaction.

But authenticity doesn't mean oversharing or rambling. It means being intentional. What part of your journey will resonate most with your audience? What tone reflects your brand's personality, are you humorous, hopeful, rebellious, refined? Think of your story not as a script, but as a compass. It guides your messaging and sets the tone for everything you communicate. A powerful story doesn't just live on your About page. It weaves through all your content from social media posts and email newsletters to packaging copy and in-person conversations. Consistency is pivotal. If your Instagram voice is cheeky and casual, but your website sounds corporate and stiff, you create dissonance. Every touch point should feel like a chapter from the same book.

Content strategy is how your story comes to life across platforms. And for small businesses, a good content strategy doesn't mean churning out constant material but it means showing up with purpose. What does your audience need to hear today? What questions are they asking? What struggles are they facing that your business can speak to, solve, or soften? This is where content becomes service, not just self-promotion. Educating, entertaining, inspiring, these are all forms of value that deepen your relationship with your audience. A coffee roaster might share brewing tips, origin stories, and staff spotlights. A boutique might showcase behind-the-scenes decisions on sourcing or offer style advice. These stories make your brand human and your content useful.

Small businesses often worry they don't have enough to say. But if you're showing up for your customers every day, you already have stories. Every satisfied client, every product launch, every tough decision carries a lesson, a moment, a message. The key is to start seeing your business not as a routine, but as a narrative in motion.

The medium matters too. Some stories are best told through visuals such as a before-and-after image, a candid behind-the-scenes video, a heartfelt customer testimonial. Others lend themselves to blog posts, email reflections, or short, snappy reels. Let your strengths and resources guide you. You don't need to master every platform, just the ones that let you communicate clearly and consistently.

Social media can amplify your story, but it must be used intentionally. The goal is not to go viral; the goal is to go deep. To create moments of connection that feels personal, not performative. Showing your face, your process, your wins and your stumbles helps audiences feel like they're part of your journey and not just observers. Email remains one of the most powerful tools in your storytelling arsenal. It's direct, intimate, and under your control unlike social media algorithms. Sharing personal notes, exclusive updates, or useful content with your subscribers builds trust and keeps your brand top of mind. Think of your email list as your inner circle, as those who've said, "I want to hear from you." Honor that relationship with value and sincerity.

When crafting your content strategy, think rhythm over volume. How often can you show up with quality? What themes can anchor your storytelling such as monthly values, seasonal focuses, customer features? Having a light structure helps prevent content fatigue and ensures you're not repeating yourself aimlessly. Storytelling is also reciprocal. Invite your customers to share their stories. Testimonials, user-generated content, and community features turn your brand into a shared experience. When people see themselves reflected in your brand, loyalty deepens.

And remember: storytelling evolves. Your brand story today may not be the same as it was when you started. That's not a failure, its growth. Share that evolution. Talk about the lessons you've learned, the pivots you've made, the insights you've gained. Transparency about the journey makes your brand feel alive, not static. Finally, great storytelling requires courage. The courage to be vulnerable, to be specific, to be real in a business world that often rewards sameness and polish. But small businesses aren't built on sameness. They're built on difference. Your voice, your perspective, your path, sincerely that is your advantage. Don't water it down. Own it.

Content strategy is not a checklist but it is a commitment. A commitment to communicate with clarity, consistency, and care. A commitment to share not just what you sell, but who you are and why it matters. When you lead with story, you lead with heart. And in a world craving authenticity, that's what people remember.

Visibility is often confused with volume these days. Many small businesses fall into the trap of chasing exposure by posting constantly, running ads everywhere, and joining every trend in the hope that visibility will automatically lead to success. But real visibility isn't just about being seen. It's about being seen by the right people, for the right reasons, and in the right context. Marketing that matters doesn't just fill feeds but it creates meaningful encounters that lead to lasting relationships.

For small businesses, the key isn't to market more, but to market smarter. With limited budgets, time, and resources, every effort must serve a purpose. The question isn't "How do I reach everyone?" but rather "How do I reach the people who actually care?" Purposeful visibility means focusing your energy on where your audience is, what they value, and how they want to be engaged.

This begins with clarity. What is the core message you want people to associate with your brand? What impression do you want to leave? When your visibility efforts are aligned with your brand identity and values, you create coherence and people recognize your voice and your vision wherever they encounter your brand. Coherence builds trust. And trust is what turns visibility into action. Choosing the right marketing channels is an essential step in building purposeful visibility. Not every business needs to be on TikTok or host webinars. Some businesses thrive through Instagram storytelling, others through SEO-driven blog content, community events, partnerships, or targeted email campaigns. The right channel is the one where your audience already spends their time and where your message naturally fits the medium.

Take social media, for instance. While it offers enormous reach, it's easy to mistake activity for impact. A thousand likes don't always translate to ten sales. Purposeful marketing on social media means treating it as a space to build brand awareness, engage in real dialogue, and tell your story in digestible, visual formats. It's not about quantity of posts but quality of presence. A thoughtful, authentic post twice a week often has more long-term value than daily noise that lacks direction.

Email marketing, often underrated, remains one of the most direct and cost-effective tools small businesses can use. It lets you communicate with people who've already expressed interest, and it gives you control over your messaging without the interference of ever-changing algorithms. But emails must offer value such as updates, insights, discounts, stories, or tips that reward the reader's attention. Search engines, meanwhile, reward businesses that answer real questions and provide useful content. A well-written blog post that helps your ideal customer solve a problem not only boosts your SEO; it positions your brand as a resource, not just a seller. Content marketing isn't about flooding the internet with information but it's about creating pieces that genuinely help, inform, or inspire.

Offline marketing often overlooked in the digital rush can be incredibly powerful for small, local businesses. Community bulletin boards, farmers' markets, local partnerships, sponsorships, and word-of-mouth still drive a significant portion of customer decisions. When visibility efforts are rooted in genuine contribution to your community, they not only elevate your brand but also deepen your roots.

Purposeful visibility also demands consistency. Marketing is not a sprint but a series of small, repeated steps that build awareness over time. That's why developing a realistic marketing calendar which is one that matches your capacity and aligns with your audience's rhythms is essential. Sporadic bursts of content followed by silence confuse your audience and undermine your credibility.

Equally important is measuring your efforts. What is working, and what isn't? Analytics can show you how many people are opening your emails, clicking your ads, visiting your site, or engaging with your content. But these numbers should be interpreted within the context of your goals. Are you looking to drive traffic, improve conversion, build brand loyalty, or increase retention? Clarity around metrics helps you refine your strategy and invest where it matters most.

One of the most overlooked aspects of visibility is repetition. Many small business owners hesitate to repeat themselves, assuming their audience will get bored. But marketing research consistently shows that people need to see a message multiple times before it sticks. Repetition, when done well, isn't redundancy rather it's reinforcement. It anchors your brand in people's minds. Still, visibility is not just external, it's also internal. How well do your employees, partners, or collaborators understand your brand and message? Can they explain what you do, who you serve, and what makes you unique? When your internal community is aligned with your external message, visibility becomes more powerful because it's reinforced at every touchpoint.

Another layer of purposeful marketing is intention over trend-chasing. Just because something is popular doesn't mean it fits your brand. Jumping on every trend can dilute your message and make your brand feel scattered or inauthentic. Instead, identify the trends that genuinely align with your mission or audience, and ignore the rest without guilt. This discernment extends to paid marketing. Running ads on Google, social media, or local outlets can be effective when done with precision. But throwing money at advertising without a clear goal or target audience is often wasteful. Before launching any campaign, ask: Who is this for? What do I want them to do? What will success look like? A well-targeted, modestly funded campaign often outperforms a broad, unfocused one.

Building visibility with purpose also means embracing patience. Real brand recognition isn't built overnight. It grows through repetition, resonance, and relationships. Show up consistently. Offer value freely. Be human in your messaging. The compound effect of these actions builds visibility that lasts. Most importantly, don't lose yourself in the process. In the pursuit of being seen, many brands forget why they started. Purposeful visibility always comes back to why you do what you do. When that purpose is clear and your actions align with it, your marketing doesn't feel like sales pitch rather it feels like an invitation. It doesn't beg for attention but it earns it.

In today's world, people aren't looking for more content. They're looking for more meaning. Your visibility is an opportunity to offer that meaning and to communicate what you stand for, who you serve, and how you make their lives better. That's not just marketing. That's leadership.

Market positioning is how your business is perceived in relation to others in your industry and how you stand out, what unique value you offer, and why customers should choose you over alternatives. Without a clear position, your brand risks blending into the background noise, making growth and sustainability elusive. Positioning begins with self-awareness. Before you can claim a space in the market, you must understand your own strengths, values, and unique offerings. What do you do better, differently, or more meaningfully than others? This isn't just about product features but it's about the total experience you create, the emotional and practical benefits you deliver, and the identity you project.

One common mistake small businesses make is trying to be everything to everyone. This approach dilutes your message and confuses your audience. Instead, effective positioning focuses on clarity and specificity. It's about choosing a niche, a segment, or a unique angle and owning it fully. When you specialize, you attract customers who resonate deeply with your focus, leading to stronger loyalty and more effective word-of-mouth.

Understanding your competitors is equally important. Conducting competitor analysis helps you identify gaps in the market and opportunities to differentiate. What are your competitors promising? Where are they succeeding, and where are they falling short? This knowledge informs your positioning strategy and helps you articulate what makes your business the better or different choice. Positioning is not static. As markets evolve and customer preferences shift, your positioning may need to adapt. But changes should be deliberate, grounded in clear insights rather than reactionary. The strongest brands evolve while maintaining their core identity, balancing innovation with consistency.

Your market position is communicated through every aspect of your brand from your logo and tagline to your website copy and customer service. Consistency across these touchpoints reinforces your position and builds trust. When customers experience your brand as coherent and reliable, your position becomes a promise fulfilled. Storytelling plays a vital role in positioning. How you tell your brand's story, what you emphasize, the tone you adopt, the values you highlight shapes perception. For example, a bakery that positions itself as an artisanal, locally sourced shop will craft stories about ingredient origins, artisan bakers, and community ties. Meanwhile, a bakery focusing on speed and convenience might emphasize ease, accessibility, and quick service.

Pricing strategy also influences positioning. Pricing too low can signal cheapness or low quality, while pricing too high can limit your audience. Positioning helps guide these decisions by aligning price with the value and experience you promise. If you position as premium, your pricing should reflect that and be supported by exceptional service or unique features. Customer experience is another powerful differentiator. Small businesses can compete by creating personal, memorable interactions that larger companies often cannot. Thoughtful packaging, handwritten thank-you notes, flexible return policies, or attentive follow-up calls all contribute to positioning your brand as caring and customer-centric.

Marketing messaging must reinforce your position with clarity and confidence. Ambiguous or generic messages dilute your brand's impact. Instead, your communications should repeatedly highlight your unique selling proposition as the reason customers should pick you. This doesn't mean constant sales pitches but weaving your positioning into every conversation and campaign.

Digital presence plays an essential role in modern positioning. Your website, social media profiles, and online reviews collectively tell your story to a vast audience. Ensuring these platforms reflect your position with authenticity and professionalism is critical. A well-crafted website with clear messaging, quality visuals, and easy navigation can elevate perception and reinforce your place in the market. Positioning also benefits from social proof. Testimonials, case studies, influencer endorsements, and media mentions all serve as evidence that you deliver on your promises. Social proof builds credibility and reduces perceived risk for potential customers, making them more likely to engage.

One overlooked element in positioning is internal alignment. Your team no matter how small must understand and embody your market position. When every employee, partner, or collaborator communicates the same message and delivers consistent experience, your positioning is strengthened exponentially. This internal clarity prevents mixed messages and builds a unified brand front. In competitive markets, niche positioning often proves most effective. By focusing on a specialized segment or unique need, small businesses can escape the pressure of competing on price alone.

Niches allow for deeper customer understanding, tailored offerings, and more effective marketing. They foster communities of loyal customers who see the brand as uniquely suited to their needs.

Embracing your uniqueness also requires confidence. It can be tempting to mimic competitors or chase trends to gain quick attention. However, customers value authenticity and consistency more than fleeting popularity. Standing tall means owning your differences and trusting that the right audience will find you. Finally, market positioning is a journey, not a destination. It evolves through trial, feedback, and refinement. Testing messaging, observing customer response, and iterating your approach helps you sharpen your position over time. Flexibility and resilience in this process ensure your brand stays relevant and compelling in an ever-changing landscape.

CHAPTER NINE
RISK AND RESILIENCE: HOW TO PLAN FOR THE UNPREDICTABLE

Every small business, regardless of size or industry, operates within a landscape peppered with uncertainties. These uncertainties, broadly known as risks, can arise from numerous sources and manifest in many forms. Understanding what risk truly means for your business and recognizing its diverse types and potential impacts is the first critical step toward building resilience and ensuring longevity.

Risk, at its core, refers to the possibility that an event or decision could lead to a loss or unfavorable outcome. For small businesses, this could translate into financial losses, operational setbacks, reputational damage, or even complete failure. Yet risk is not inherently negative. It's the inherent uncertainty of business life which is an element to be managed, mitigated, and, when possible, leveraged for advantage. One of the challenges small business owners face is the invisible nature of many risks. Unlike visible operational tasks such as inventory management or marketing, risks often lurk beneath the surface, unnoticed until they trigger a crisis. This is why a proactive understanding of risk is indispensable by not just reacting to problems as they arise but anticipating and preparing for them.

Risks can be broadly categorized into several types, each carrying distinct characteristics and implications. Financial Risks are among the most immediate and tangible. These include cash flow shortages, credit issues, fluctuating sales, unexpected expenses, or debt obligations that strain resources. A sudden drop in revenue, an unpaid invoice, or an unforeseen equipment repair can quickly jeopardize operations if financial buffers are weak. For small businesses, where margins are often tight, financial risks require vigilant monitoring and agile responses.

Operational Risks relate to disruptions in the day-to-day functioning of the business. These might stem from supply chain interruptions, equipment failures, employee absences, or technology breakdowns. For example, if a key supplier suddenly halts deliveries or a software glitch compromises your point-of-sale system, your ability to serve customers and generate income can be compromised. Small businesses often lack the redundancy systems of larger enterprises, making operational risks particularly acute. Market Risks involve changes in the broader business environment such as shifts in customer preferences, emerging competitors, regulatory changes, or economic downturns. These risks can erode demand for your products or services or increase the cost of doing business. For instance, a new competitor entering your local market with aggressive pricing or a change in industry regulations can create new challenges that demand rapid adaptation.

Reputational Risks arise when the public perception of your business suffers. This might be due to poor customer service, product failures, negative reviews, or social media missteps. For small businesses, reputation is often one of their most valuable assets, built through close customer relationships and community trust. Damage to this can have long-lasting effects, potentially shrinking your customer base or limiting future opportunities. Legal and Compliance Risks involve failing to meet regulatory requirements, such as tax obligations, labor laws, health and safety standards, or intellectual property protections. Non-compliance can result in fines, lawsuits, or forced closure. Small business owners often juggle multiple responsibilities and may overlook or misunderstand complex regulations, increasing exposure to legal risks.

Beyond these categories, risks can also be external or internal. External risks come from outside the business such as natural disasters, economic crises, political instability, or pandemics. These are largely uncontrollable but can be anticipated and planned for. Internal risks originate within the business, such as poor management decisions, employee turnover, or security breaches. Both require distinct strategies for mitigation.

Understanding the impacts of risk is as important as identifying the risks themselves. Not every risk carries the same weight or likelihood. Some risks, while severe in consequence, may have a low chance of occurrence. Others may be frequent but manageable. Effective risk management requires assessing both probability and impact, enabling prioritization of efforts. The ripple effects of risk can extend beyond immediate losses. Financial strain can hinder growth opportunities; operational disruptions may damage customer trust; reputational hits can reduce market share; legal troubles can drain resources and focus. Small businesses are especially vulnerable to cascading impacts because they often operate with limited buffers and lean staffing.

Yet, embracing risk with awareness transforms it from a looming threat into a manageable reality. It empowers small business owners to make informed decisions, allocate resources wisely, and cultivates a mindset that sees challenges as part of the entrepreneurial journey and not reasons to retreat. Recognizing risk also opens pathways to innovation and growth. Calculated risks, taken thoughtfully, can lead to breakthroughs, new markets, and competitive advantage. Understanding risk fully means not just avoiding danger, but seizing opportunities with eyes wide open.

Ultimately, a deep comprehension of the types and impacts of risk lays the foundation for every subsequent step in building a resilient business. It prepares you to build financial buffers, design contingency plans, secure insurance protections, and foster a culture of adaptability. It shifts risk from a shadowy, paralyzing force to a visible, navigable terrain where careful planning and strategic action prevail. By embracing risk as an integral part of business life and as something to understand, anticipate, and address, you position yourself and your business to weather uncertainty with confidence and clarity.

Financial buffers serve as the critical safety nets that catch you when unforeseen events strike. Whether it's a sudden drop in sales, an unexpected repair bill, or a delay in payment from clients, having accessible financial resources can mean the difference between weathering a storm and facing collapse. Building and managing these buffers is an essential pillar of resilience and long-term success.

Financial buffers come in several forms, the most fundamental being savings. Much like personal finance, businesses benefit immensely from setting aside reserves specifically earmarked for emergencies. These funds should ideally cover several months of fixed expenses such as rent, salaries, utilities, providing a cushion during lean periods. However, building such savings requires discipline and foresight, particularly for small businesses where every dollar counts. It means prioritizing cash flow management, controlling unnecessary expenses, and sometimes making tough decisions about investments or growth pace.

Closely linked to savings is the effective management of cash flow which is the lifeblood of any business. Cash flow management is about more than just tracking income and expenses; it's about forecasting future inflows and outflows, identifying potential shortfalls before they become crises, and proactively addressing them. For example, understanding seasonal trends, negotiating better payment terms with suppliers, or encouraging early payments from customers can significantly improve cash availability. Credit plays a pivotal role as well, serving as a financial buffer that can be tapped when cash reserves are insufficient. Establishing good relationships with lenders, securing lines of credit, or maintaining business credit cards provide additional flexibility. However, credit must be used judiciously; high-interest debt or overreliance can quickly compound financial risks. The key is balancing access to credit with prudent repayment plans and transparent financial tracking.

Another powerful tool for building financial resilience is creating diversified revenue streams. Relying too heavily on a single client, product, or market can expose your business to sharp shocks if that source dries up. By broadening your income base, you create internal buffers that stabilize overall cash flow, making it easier to absorb localized risks.

Financial buffers are not static. Regular review and adjustment are necessary to reflect changing business realities whether it's growth requiring larger reserves or contraction calling for cost realignment. Maintaining financial discipline in good times ensures preparedness for bad times. Technology can be a valuable ally in managing finances. Modern accounting software, budgeting apps, and cash flow forecasting tools help small business owners visualize their financial position clearly and make informed decisions swiftly. They reduce the chance of oversight and free up mental bandwidth for strategic thinking. Importantly, building financial buffers is as much a mindset as it is a set of practices. It requires embracing prudence without stifling ambition, balancing caution with calculated risk-taking. Many successful entrepreneurs credit their resilience not just to financial resources but to the mental preparedness that buffers and provide confidence to face uncertainty without panic.

In practice, building financial buffers starts with setting clear financial goals and metrics. How much cash reserve is adequate for your business size and sector? What credit options are realistic and sustainable? What cash flow patterns demand attention? Answering these questions with data and experience guides effective buffer creation.

Financial buffers also extend beyond cash and credit. Inventory management, for example, can act as a buffer when done strategically. Excess stock ties up cash but insufficient stock can halt sales. Finding the right balance ensures smooth operations without unnecessary financial strain. Moreover, it's crucial to keep business and personal finances separate. Mixing these can obscure true financial health and complicate buffer management. Clear accounting boundaries facilitate accurate tracking and better financial decision-making. Ultimately, building robust financial buffers is an ongoing process of learning, adjusting, and reinforcing. It prepares your business not just to survive the unpredictable but to emerge stronger. With solid financial foundations, you gain the agility to seize new opportunities and the peace of mind to focus on growth.

In the life of a small business, the unexpected is not a question of if, but when. Natural disasters, supply chain disruptions, technology failures, sudden shifts in market demand, or even personal emergencies can strike with little warning and threaten your business's stability. Contingency planning is the proactive strategy that transforms uncertainty from a paralyzing threat into a manageable challenge. It equips small business owners with clear, actionable steps to respond effectively when unforeseen events occur, ensuring continuity, minimizing damage, and speeding recovery. At its essence, contingency planning is about foresight and preparation. It involves identifying potential risks, imagining plausible scenarios, and crafting specific responses to maintain critical operations under adverse conditions. This is not about fearing the worst but preparing intelligently so your business can survive and thrive despite setbacks.

The first step in building a contingency plan is to conduct a thorough risk assessment. This means systematically analyzing your business environment to pinpoint vulnerabilities. What events could disrupt your supply chain? What internal processes are most sensitive to failure? Which customer segments or revenue streams are at greatest risk? What external forces such as economic, regulatory, natural could impact your operations? This assessment should be realistic, inclusive, and informed by both historical data and forward-looking trends.

Once risks are identified, prioritize them based on likelihood and potential impact. Not every risk demands the same level of attention; some may be rare but catastrophic, while others might be frequent yet manageable. Prioritization helps allocate resources effectively and ensures that the most critical threats receive detailed planning. The next phase is scenario development. For each prioritized risk, envision plausible "what if" situations. For example, if your primary supplier suddenly halts deliveries, what alternative sources can you tap? If a key employee falls ill or leaves abruptly, how will you maintain essential functions? What happens if a natural disaster damages your physical premises? Scenario planning pushes beyond abstract risk lists to concrete, actionable situations that test your readiness.

Based on these scenarios, develop contingency strategies. These are the specific steps your business will take to respond and adapt. Contingency strategies often include backup plans, resource reallocation, communication protocols, and temporary operational adjustments. The goal is to minimize disruption, protect customers and employees, and preserve core business functions.

A critical component of contingency planning is communication. Clear, timely communication both internally and externally can dramatically influence outcomes during crises. Internally, everyone involved should understand their roles and responsibilities under the contingency plan. Externally, keeping customers, suppliers, and stakeholders informed builds trust and manages expectations. Effective communication prevents panic, misinformation, and operational confusion.

Testing your contingency plans through drills or simulations is essential. Like emergency fire drills, these exercises reveal gaps, inefficiencies, or misunderstandings in your plan. Testing also builds confidence among team members and ensures that when real disruptions occur, responses are swift and coordinated. Many small businesses overlook this step, only to find plans fall short in actual emergencies. Technology plays a pivotal role in contingency planning. Cloud-based systems, data backups, remote work capabilities, and communication platforms enhance your ability to maintain operations during disruptions. Ensuring that your digital infrastructure is resilient and accessible is part of a modern contingency strategy.

Financial preparedness intertwines closely with contingency planning. Beyond cash reserves and credit lines, it's vital to assess the financial implications of potential disruptions. How long can your business sustain reduced revenue? What fixed costs can be deferred or renegotiated? Contingency budgeting ensures that funds are available not only for daily operations but also for emergency response.

Legal and regulatory considerations should also be integrated into contingency plans. Ensure compliance with safety regulations, data protection laws, and contractual obligations even in disrupted scenarios. Review contracts for force majeure clauses and understand your liabilities and protections. Beyond formal plans and resources, building a culture of flexibility and problem-solving mindset among yourself and your team is crucial. Contingency planning is not a one-time task but a continuous practice embedded in daily decision-making and organizational culture. Encouraging creativity, collaboration, and calm under pressure prepares your business to navigate uncertainty more smoothly. Contingency planning also requires collaboration with external partners. Your suppliers, service providers, financial institutions, and even local authorities can be critical allies during disruptions. Establishing strong relationships and clear expectations before a crisis enhances coordination and support when you need it most.

Documentation is an often overlooked but vital aspect of contingency planning. Keep your plans written, accessible, and regularly updated. Document who is responsible for what actions, key contacts, and step-by-step procedures. Clear documentation transforms plans from abstract concepts into practical roadmaps.

Remember, contingency planning is not about predicting every possible event but preparing to adapt rapidly and effectively to whatever comes your way. Flexibility is key. As you learn from experience and changing circumstances, your plans should evolve.

The benefits of solid contingency planning extend far beyond crisis management. They build confidence for you and your teams, reassure customers and partners, and create a foundation for sustainable growth. Knowing you can handle setbacks without losing momentum frees you to take calculated risks and innovate. In the unpredictable world of small business, contingency planning is the armor that shields you from the unexpected. It turns vulnerability into strength and uncertainty into opportunity. By committing time and effort to thoughtful planning, testing, and continuous improvement, you ensure your business is ready not just to survive challenges but to emerge stronger on the other side.

While planning and financial buffers provide vital layers of defense, no strategy is complete without addressing risk through insurance and legal protections. These tools offer a structured way to transfer, reduce, or manage risks that could otherwise cause catastrophic damage. Understanding and implementing appropriate insurance coverage and legal safeguards is not merely a regulatory checkbox as it is a fundamental part of responsible business stewardship that protects assets, reputation, and future viability.

Insurance operates on the principle of risk transfer. By paying a premium, a business shifts the financial burden of certain risks to an insurer. This provides a safety net that can absorb shocks from events such as accidents, property damage, lawsuits, or business interruptions. For small businesses, the right insurance coverage can mean the difference between recovery and closure in the wake of unexpected events. However, insurance is not one-size-fits-all. The variety of policies available can be overwhelming, and selecting coverage requires a clear understanding of your business's unique risks. Common insurance types that small businesses should consider include several factors.

General Liability Insurance covers claims related to bodily injury, property damage, and personal injury that occur on business premises or due to business operations. This protects against lawsuits and legal costs arising from accidents or negligence. Property Insurance safeguards physical assets such as buildings, equipment, inventory, and furnishings against risks like fire, theft, or natural disasters. Business interruption insurance which helps to provide income replacement if your business operations are halted due to a covered event, helping to cover ongoing expenses during downtime. Professional liability insurance (Errors and Omissions) which helps to protects service providers from claims of negligence, mistakes, or failure to deliver promised services. Workers' Compensation Insurance which is mandated in many regions, this covers medical expenses and lost wages if employees are injured on the job. Cyber Liability Insurance is increasingly important for businesses reliant on digital systems, this protects against data breaches, cyberattacks, and related liabilities.

Choosing appropriate insurance coverage involves assessing both the likelihood and impact of various risks, balanced against premium costs. Consulting with insurance professionals, comparing policies, and regularly reviewing coverage as your business evolves are critical steps.

Legal protections complement insurance by establishing the rules and frameworks that govern your business operations and relationships. These safeguards help prevent disputes, clarify responsibilities, and limit liabilities. Contracts are essential legal tools that define terms, obligations, and dispute resolution mechanisms with customers, suppliers, employees, and partners. Well-drafted contracts reduce misunderstandings and provide clear recourse in case of breach or conflict. Small business owners should invest time in creating and reviewing contracts tailored to their specific needs, and consider legal counsel for complex agreements.

Compliance with regulatory requirements also serves as legal protection. Understanding and adhering to laws related to taxes, employment, health and safety, intellectual property, and environmental standards prevents costly fines and legal action. Keeping current with regulatory changes and seeking expert advice helps avoid inadvertent violations. Intellectual property (IP) protections, including trademarks, copyrights, and patents, safeguard your brand identity, creative works, and inventions. Registering IP rights prevents unauthorized use or imitation, preserving competitive advantage. Dispute resolution mechanisms such as mediation, arbitration, or litigation are part of legal readiness. Having clear procedures in place ensures that conflicts are managed efficiently and with minimal disruption.

Document retention and recordkeeping are vital legal practices. Maintaining accurate financial records, contracts, licenses, and correspondence supports compliance, protects rights, and facilitates defense in case of audits or disputes. Small business owners often underestimate the importance of these legal protections until they face a crisis. Proactive legal risk management reduces vulnerabilities, enhances credibility, and contributes to business stability. Integrating insurance and legal safeguards into your overall risk management strategy creates a comprehensive defense network. It enables you to face uncertainty with confidence, knowing that financial, operational, and legal risks are addressed systematically. Furthermore, insurance and legal protections foster trust among customers, partners, and employees. Demonstrating that your business operates with professionalism and responsibility can be a competitive differentiator.

Regularly reviewing your insurance policies and legal documents ensures they remain aligned with your evolving business needs. Changes in operations, growth, or market conditions may necessitate adjustments to maintain adequate protection. Ultimately, investing in insurance and legal safeguards is an investment in the sustainability and reputation of your business. It reflects a mature approach to entrepreneurship and one that balances ambition with prudence and risk with resilience. By understanding and applying these tools thoughtfully, small business owners can transform potential liabilities into manageable components of a robust risk management framework. This empowers you not only to survive challenges but to build a foundation for enduring success.

In the dynamic environment of small business, the only constant is change. New technologies emerge, markets evolve, consumer behaviors shift, and regulatory landscapes transform. Alongside these changes come new risks, some anticipated, others surprising. Continuous monitoring and adaptation is the final, yet critical, piece in the puzzle of effective risk management and resilience. It's the ongoing process that enables small business owners to detect emerging threats early, respond proactively, and ensure their enterprise remains agile and robust in the face of uncertainty.

Risk is not static; it fluctuates as internal and external conditions change. What was once a minor concern can become a significant threat overnight, while previously high-risk issues may fade into the background. Without regular vigilance, businesses risk being caught off guard, reacting late and inefficiently. Continuous monitoring is about establishing systems and habits that keep risk visibility high and responses timely.

The first step in continuous monitoring is cultivating a risk-aware culture within the business. This means fostering an environment where employees at all levels understand the importance of risk management, feel responsible for identifying potential issues, and communicate concerns openly. Encouraging transparency and collaboration transforms risk management from a solitary task of the owner or manager into a shared priority, increasing the likelihood of early detection and swift action. Technology plays a vital role in enabling ongoing risk monitoring. Advances in data analytics, real-time reporting, and artificial intelligence allow small businesses to track key performance indicators, financial health, market trends, and operational anomalies continuously. For example, software can flag unusual fluctuations in cash flow, detect cybersecurity threats, or monitor supplier reliability. Leveraging these tools provides objective, timely insights that inform decision-making.

External monitoring is equally important. Staying informed about changes in laws and regulations, industry developments, competitor activities, and broader economic conditions helps businesses anticipate and prepare for risks before they materialize. Subscribing to industry newsletters, joining professional networks, and engaging with local business associations are practical ways to maintain this awareness. Scenario planning and stress testing, initially done during contingency planning, should be revisited regularly as part of continuous adaptation. Running "what-if" analyses against new data and circumstances reveals fresh vulnerabilities and tests the robustness of existing plans. This iterative process ensures your risk response remains relevant and effective.

Adaptation requires flexibility, not just in plans but in mindset. Small business owners must be willing to pivot strategies, adjust operations, and reallocate resources as new information emerges. This agility often distinguishes thriving businesses from those that falter when faced with change. Financial agility is particularly crucial. Maintaining updated cash flow forecasts, revisiting budgets, and adjusting credit lines in response to emerging risks helps preserve financial stability. Likewise, operational adjustments such as diversifying suppliers, altering marketing strategies, or upgrading technology support resilience.

Communication channels established during contingency planning should be kept active and refined. Regularly updating employees, customers, and partners about changes in risk posture or business operations builds trust and preparedness. Transparent dialogue also invites feedback and insights that can enhance risk management efforts.

Continuous training and development reinforce risk awareness and capability. Investing in skill-building around areas like cybersecurity, compliance, and crisis management equips your team to respond competently and confidently. Documentation remains a cornerstone of monitoring and adaptation. Keeping detailed records of risk assessments, incidents, responses, and lessons learned creates an institutional memory that informs future actions. It also supports accountability and continuous improvement.

It's important to remember that continuous monitoring is not about eliminating risk which is an impossible goal but about managing it intelligently and dynamically. Risk is an inherent part of entrepreneurship, and learning to live with it while steering your business safely through challenges is a mark of true mastery. Small businesses often operate with limited resources, making it tempting to treat risk management as a one-time task. However, those who embed continuous monitoring and adaptation into their operations gain a powerful edge. They avoid costly surprises, capitalize on emerging opportunities, and build resilience that sustains long-term success.

In today's interconnected and fast-moving world, the pace of change will only accelerate. Businesses that rest on yesterday's plans risk obsolescence. By contrast, those who commit to vigilance and flexibility position themselves to lead and innovate. Continuous monitoring and adaptation foster a proactive rather than reactive approach. They cultivate confidence and with that confidence, your business can navigate uncertainty, recover from setbacks, and seize new horizons. This mindset transforms risk from a threat into a catalyst for growth and evolution.

CHAPTER TEN

SCALING SMART: GROWTH THAT DOESN'T BREAK WHAT YOU HAVE BUILT

Scaling a small business is one of the most exciting yet challenging milestones an entrepreneur can face. It promises growth, increased revenue, and the opportunity to reach new customers or markets. But it also brings risks such as complexity, stretched resources, and potential loss of control. Knowing when to scale is a nuanced decision that requires both keen observation and disciplined analysis. It's about identifying clear, reliable signals that your business is prepared for expansion and avoiding the pitfalls of premature scaling that can threaten everything you've built.

At its core, recognizing the right time to scale begins with a deep understanding of your current business performance and capacity. Growth is not merely about increasing sales or customer numbers; it's about ensuring your business model, operations, finances, and people can handle that growth sustainably. Without this foundation, scaling can quickly lead to operational breakdowns, quality decline, and financial strain.

One of the most obvious indicators that your business may be ready to scale is consistent, growing demand for your product or service. This isn't just a spike in sales due to seasonal factors or one-off events but sustained interest reflected in increasing orders, repeat customers, and expanding market reach. When demand consistently outpaces your current capacity to deliver, it signals the need to expand resources, whether through hiring, production, or infrastructure. Closely linked to demand is the stability and predictability of your business operations. Before scaling, you want to have repeatable, reliable processes in place that produce consistent results. If your current workflows depend heavily on manual effort, individual heroics, or ad hoc problem-solving, scaling will magnify inefficiencies and errors. Businesses that have standardized operations, clear documentation, and a culture of continuous improvement are much better positioned to grow without losing quality or control.

Financial readiness is equally critical. Scaling often requires upfront investment whether in inventory, staffing, marketing, or technology. You should have a clear picture of your cash flow, profit margins, and financial reserves. Importantly, your business should be profitable or at least have a viable path to profitability with scaling. Operating on thin margins or unstable finances makes expansion risky and can lead to cash crunches or debt.

Equally important is having the right team and leadership in place. Growth demands more from your people both in terms of capacity and skills. Before scaling, assess whether your current team can manage increased workloads and complexities or if you need to bring in new talent with specific expertise. Additionally, your leadership must be ready to shift from day-to-day hands-on management to strategic oversight, delegating operational tasks and focusing on vision and growth.

Customer feedback is another valuable signal. Loyal, satisfied customers who not only repeat purchases but also refer others can be a strong indicator that your product or service meets a genuine market need. Positive reviews, high retention rates, and low customer complaints all suggest a solid foundation on which to build.

Market conditions also influence timing. External factors like industry growth trends, competitor movements, economic climate, and technological advancements can either accelerate or caution against scaling. For example, entering a growing market or riding a technological wave can provide opportunities to scale quickly. Conversely, an economic downturn or regulatory uncertainty might advise a more cautious approach. It's also essential to evaluate your competitive advantage. Do you have a unique value proposition or differentiators that set you apart? Can these be maintained or enhanced as you grow? Scaling without a defensible position risks diluting your brand or losing market share to competitors.

While these signals help identify readiness, the decision to scale should also consider your personal goals and risk tolerance as a business owner. Growth brings greater responsibility, complexity, and often stress. Be honest about whether you're prepared mentally and emotionally for the demands of a larger operation. One common trap is scaling too early, driven by excitement, external pressure, or the mistaken belief that bigger is always better. Premature scaling often leads to cash flow problems, quality issues, and operational chaos, ultimately forcing retrenchment or failure. The key is measured growth and scaling only when your business fundamentals are solid and you have a clear plan to manage expansion. To avoid missteps, consider piloting growth initiatives on a smaller scale first. Test new markets, increase production in phases, or launch targeted marketing campaigns to validate assumptions and refine your approach. This incremental scaling reduces risk and builds confidence.

Recognizing the right time to scale requires a balanced view of your business's internal readiness, market conditions, and personal preparedness. It's a strategic decision grounded in data, operational strength, financial health, and vision. By waiting for the right signals and approaching growth deliberately, you preserve the integrity of what you've built and position your business for sustainable success.

Growth is often seen as the ultimate validation of a business's success. It brings with it the allure of new customers, increased revenue, and greater market influence. Yet, expansion also brings risk not just in logistics or finance, but in the potential erosion of the very qualities that made the business succeed in the first place. For small businesses especially, the strength of their identity, culture, customer relationships, and operational discipline is often what sets them apart from larger, more impersonal competitors. Preserving these core strengths during periods of growth isn't simply desirable, it's essential.

As a business expands, complexity increases. New employees come on board, new systems are introduced, and new markets are entered. Each of these changes can strain or dilute the foundational values and practices that defined the business in its earlier stages. What once relied on the tight-knit understanding between a founder and a small team must now be translated into processes, structures, and behaviors that scale. Without this intentional translation, businesses often find themselves growing in size while shrinking in identity.

At the heart of core preservation is clarity. Business owners must have a clear understanding of what their core strengths actually are. This goes beyond a general sense of "what works" to a specific articulation of the values, processes, and unique differentiators that have driven success to date. Is it your deep customer intimacy and personalized service? A tightly honed operational process that delivers speed and quality? A distinctive brand voice that resonates with a specific niche? Pinpointing these elements is the first step toward protecting them.

This clarity then needs to be deliberately embedded into every aspect of the business. As new people join, onboarding processes must do more than teach job duties as they must instill the values and ethos that define the culture. As teams grow, leadership must reinforce the importance of these principles through both communication and example. Organizational culture cannot be left to chance. It must be nurtured, communicated, and modeled consistently.

Operational excellence which is another key strength also faces risks during expansion. Processes that worked for a team of five may buckle under the weight of twenty. Systems that tracked customer needs manually might fail when serving ten times the volume.

Preserving excellence means recognizing where systems need to evolve while ensuring that the core intentions such as efficiency, quality, and attention to detail remain intact. Scaling operations is not about replacing old processes blindly but refining and enhancing them for larger scale without sacrificing their essence.

This is where documentation and standardization become invaluable. What was once transmitted through proximity and repetition must now be written down, shared widely, and reviewed regularly. Documenting workflows, best practices, and customer interaction protocols ensures that your business's way of doing things becomes a shared language, not a fading memory. But this standardization should never become rigidity. The goal is consistency with room for judgment and improvement, not bureaucratic stagnation.

Leadership style also evolves with growth, and here lies a potential threat to your culture. As more layers are added to the organization, the direct influence of the founder or early leadership naturally diminishes. Preserving the tone and decision-making philosophy requires developing leaders who share and can transmit the same values. Investing in leadership development especially promoting from within where possible helps ensure continuity. A consistent tone from top to bottom reinforces your business identity and supports cultural cohesion.

Customer relationships are another area at risk during expansion. In the early stages, small business owners often know their customers personally. This intimacy fosters loyalty, trust, and a deep understanding of needs. As the customer base grows, that personal touch can be difficult to scale. The danger lies in becoming transactional, where customers feel like numbers rather than valued individuals. To preserve this strength, businesses must invest in systems that allow personalized service at scale such as CRM tools, feedback loops, and empowered frontline employees who are trained and trusted to go the extra mile.

Equally important is maintaining a feedback-driven culture. When businesses are small, feedback often flows informally and immediately. Employees talk to each other, and leaders are close to the action. In larger organizations, these lines can blur. To preserve agility and responsiveness, feedback mechanisms must be formalized without becoming impersonal. Regular team check-ins, anonymous surveys, customer interviews, and open-door policies help keep communication flowing and issues visible.

Brand integrity is another core strength vulnerable to dilution as businesses expand. With more marketing channels, product lines, or geographic locations, it's easy to lose consistency in voice, message, or values. Protecting your brand means developing clear guidelines and maintaining a disciplined approach to brand presentation. Every new hire, every advertisement, and every customer interaction should reflect the same brand personality. Consistency builds trust, and trust sustains loyalty during growth. Preserving core strengths also involves making tough choices about what not to do. Every opportunity for growth must be measured against its impact on your foundational strengths. Will chasing a new market force you to change your product in a way that compromises quality? Will scaling too fast make it harder to maintain your unique service approach? Strategic restraint and knowing when to say no is as important as seizing opportunities.

Technology can both support and threaten core strengths. On one hand, it enables scalability, efficiency, and data-driven decisions. On the other, it can create distance between people and processes if not used thoughtfully. Choose tools that enhance rather than replace human connection. Automate repetitive tasks so employees can focus on what matters most such as building relationships, solving problems, and innovating. Another essential piece is alignment. As your business grows, everyone from the newest intern to senior leadership must remain aligned around a shared mission. This means revisiting your vision regularly, communicating it clearly, and tying everyday actions back to it. Alignment creates cohesion across departments, minimizes internal conflict, and ensures that growth efforts are moving in the same direction.

Finally, preserving your entrepreneurial spirit is perhaps the most intangible but vital core strength. It's the mindset that drives initiative, creativity, and adaptability. As a business grows, the risk is that processes and hierarchies dampen this spirit. Cultivating an environment that encourages innovation, recognizes contribution, and rewards risk-taking keeps the business alive and dynamic even as it matures. In the end, scaling smartly means protecting the roots while growing the branches. It's about evolving without forgetting who you are. Businesses that grow without losing their soul become not only larger but stronger. They inspire deeper loyalty, perform more reliably, and adapt more gracefully.

Sustainable growth requires strategic foresight particularly in how a company positions itself as it enters new markets or targets new customer segments. Market expansion without a clear positioning strategy can lead to resource overextension, loss of brand identity, and eventual market retreat. Strategic market positioning for new horizons is about ensuring that expansion is both meaningful and sustainable, preserving the brand's essence while tapping into new opportunities.

Strategic positioning is more than just placing a product on a shelf or launching a new marketing campaign. It encompasses how a company defines its value proposition, how it communicates its uniqueness, and how it aligns its operations to deliver on its brand promise in unfamiliar territories. As businesses set their sights on broader horizons whether entering international markets, targeting new demographics, or offering innovative products, they must do so with careful planning and a nuanced understanding of both the risks and opportunities involved.

Strategic market positioning refers to the deliberate process by which a company identifies its niche in a new or evolving market. It involves articulating what the brand stands for, who its target customers are, and how it distinguishes itself from competitors. Unlike basic marketing tactics, which often focus on short-term promotion and visibility, strategic positioning has a long-term focus. It seeks to create a distinct place in the consumer's mind, one that remains consistent even as markets change. Effective positioning aligns with a company's core mission and values, ensuring that every move into a new market is an extension not a departure of its established identity. This coherence is critical not only for maintaining internal focus but also for sustaining consumer trust. In an age where customers are increasingly value-driven, any misalignment between a brand's messaging and its market actions can quickly erode credibility.

Before stepping into new markets, businesses must conduct an honest assessment of their readiness. Growth is enticing, but it must be pursued with a strong foundation in place. Internally, the company should evaluate its operational capacity, financial stability, and leadership bandwidth. Does it have the systems and people in place to support new operations without compromising existing ones? Can it handle increased complexity in supply chains, customer service, and compliance requirements?

Operational readiness is equally critical. Companies must ensure that they can meet the expectations of a new market in terms of product quality, delivery timelines, and customer engagement. Entering a market with subpar execution not only risks failure in that segment but can also tarnish the brand's reputation in its core markets. Cultural readiness also plays a role. As companies expand into diverse geographic or demographic markets, they must ensure that their teams are equipped to navigate cultural nuances, adapt communication styles, and manage cross-cultural teams. Strategic market positioning is as much about internal alignment as it is about external messaging.

Not every growth opportunity is the right one. Identifying which markets to enter should be a strategic decision grounded in data and aligned with long-term goals. This involves conducting thorough market research to understand demand, customer behavior, competitive landscape, and regulatory environments. More importantly, the new market should complement the company's strengths. A technology firm known for its premium products may struggle to compete in price-sensitive emerging markets unless it adjusts its model or develops localized solutions. Similarly, a brand celebrated for its ethical sourcing in Europe might face scrutiny if it enters markets where transparency is lacking.

By aligning market selection with the company's values and capabilities, businesses can ensure more coherent and sustainable expansion. This alignment also allows for more effective positioning when a company enters a market with a clear understanding of its differentiators, it can tailor its messaging to resonate deeply with local consumers.

Perhaps the most common pitfall in expansion is brand dilution. In the rush to appeal to new audiences, companies may stretch their brand messaging too far, losing the clarity that made them successful in the first place. Strategic positioning requires a balance between adaptation and consistency. To maintain brand integrity, businesses should define non-negotiable elements of their identity such as core values, tone of voice, visual branding, and customer promise that must remain consistent across all markets. At the same time, they can adapt secondary elements to suit local preferences. For example, while the tone and visuals may stay constant, product offerings or promotional channels might differ depending on cultural norms.

The key is to ensure that every market perceives the brand as relevant yet authentic. This requires cross-functional collaboration between marketing, product development, and customer service teams to deliver a unified but locally adapted experience. Once a business has assessed its readiness and identified target markets, the next step is determining the best entry strategy. There is no one-size-fits-all approach. The right method depends on the market characteristics, the company's objectives, and its available resources. Generally, companies can expand into new segments or geographies through organic growth, partnerships, joint ventures, acquisitions, or franchising.

Organic growth which is entering the market from scratch with in-house resources offers maximum control and brand fidelity. However, it is typically slower and requires significant upfront investment. This method works best for businesses that have a clear understanding of the new market and are confident in their ability to deliver value without local partners. Strategic partnerships or joint ventures, on the other hand, allow companies to collaborate with established local players. This reduces entry risk, accelerates market penetration, and brings local expertise into the fold. However, it requires careful alignment of values, business models, and long-term goals to avoid conflict and brand confusion.

Acquisitions provide immediate access to market share, infrastructure, and customer bases. When executed properly, they can fast-track growth and solidify market presence. But acquisitions also carry risks: integration challenges, cultural clashes, and brand inconsistency can all undermine strategic positioning. Franchising and licensing offer lower-risk entry into new markets, particularly in the consumer sector. These models allow businesses to expand without significant capital investment, but they require rigorous quality control and brand governance systems to ensure the brand experience remains consistent across operators.

Regardless of the entry strategy, localization is key. This does not mean changing the brand's core identity, but rather tailoring products, communication, and service delivery to meet local expectations. For instance, a global restaurant chain might keep its logo and brand promise but localize its menu to reflect regional tastes. Effective localization strengthens the connection between the brand and the target audience while preserving strategic integrity.

Market expansion is an exciting phase, but it also presents significant risks, many of which stem from poor planning or over-ambition. One of the most frequent mistakes is overextension. Companies often attempt to grow too quickly, entering multiple markets simultaneously without sufficient infrastructure, capital, or human resources. This can strain operations and dilute strategic focus, making it difficult to maintain quality or responsiveness.

Another common pitfall is neglecting the core market. While pursuing new opportunities, companies may inadvertently ignore their original customer base. This can lead to declining loyalty and revenue in established markets, effectively cancelling out any gains from expansion. A successful growth strategy ensures continued investment in core operations, even while branching into new areas. Underestimating competitive dynamics is also dangerous. Just because a product or service is successful in one region does not guarantee it will succeed elsewhere. Local competitors often have deep insights into customer behavior, regulatory environments, and supply chains. Without comprehensive competitive analysis, newcomers may find themselves outmaneuvered by more agile or better-informed rivals.

Finally, companies must be wary of cultural misalignment. Even well-intentioned marketing campaigns or product launches can backfire if they fail to respect cultural norms or values. Businesses must invest in local expertise and be willing to listen and adapt not just translate their existing strategies, but transform them as needed to resonate authentically in new contexts.

To manage a successful market expansion, businesses need clear metrics to evaluate performance. These key performance indicators (KPIs) should align with the goals of the strategic positioning effort. Common KPIs include market share growth, customer acquisition cost, customer lifetime value, brand recognition, and net promoter score (NPS). For digital ventures, engagement metrics such as website traffic, conversion rates, and social media sentiment can offer valuable insights.

However, numbers alone are not enough. Companies must also build feedback loops to capture qualitative data from customers, partners, and employees. These insights are essential for understanding how the brand is perceived and where adjustments are needed. Continuous learning and adaptation are hallmarks of successful market expansion. Moreover, businesses should be prepared to pivot or pull back if results consistently fall short. Strategic flexibility is not a sign of failure rather it's a sign of resilience and long-term thinking. Companies that are willing to recalibrate their approach based on real-world feedback are more likely to succeed in the long run. An often-overlooked aspect of measuring success is the long-term brand impact. A market entry that generates short-term profits but compromises brand equity or operational integrity can do more harm than good. Strategic market positioning should always prioritize the longevity of the brand, ensuring that every expansion strengthens—not undermines—its core value proposition.

Strategic market positioning for new horizons is a complex yet rewarding endeavor. It requires a deep understanding of the company's core identity, a disciplined approach to market selection, and a well-thought-out entry strategy that balances control with adaptability. Above all, it demands consistency ensuring that as the brand reaches new customers and geographies, it does so without losing the essence that made it successful in the first place. Growth should never come at the cost of strategic clarity. By investing in thoughtful positioning, companies can expand in a way that not only increases market share but also enhances their reputation, customer loyalty, and long-term viability. In a world of constant change, strategic market positioning is not just a growth strategy but it is a survival strategy.

Final Note

Small-scale businesses are the heartbeat of economic resilience, innovation, and local empowerment. Throughout this book, I have shared lessons drawn from hands-on experience including mistakes, breakthroughs, and insights that I hope illuminate your path as a current or aspiring entrepreneur.

As you step forward, remember that success doesn't come from following a perfect plan but from having the courage to start, the discipline to persist, and the humility to keep learning. May this book serve as both compass and companion on your entrepreneurial journey.

Thank you for reading.
— *Elvis Gboji Ajai*

Further Reading: Recommended Books

For those eager to dive deeper into the world of small business, these six books offer timeless wisdom, practical strategies, and real-world inspiration:

1. **"The Lean Startup"** by *Eric Ries*
   — A revolutionary approach to launching and managing startups through rapid experimentation.

2. **"The E-Myth Revisited"** by *Michael E. Gerber*
   — A classic that demystifies the myths around starting and running a small business effectively.

3. **"Start Small, Stay Small"** by *Rob Walling*
   — A guide for solo entrepreneurs and bootstrappers looking to build a profitable business without outside funding.

4. **"Company of One"** by *Paul Jarvis*
   — A compelling case for why staying small might be the smartest path to business success.

5. **"Rework"** by *Jason Fried and David Heinemeier Hansson*
   — Unconventional yet deeply practical insights from the founders of Basecamp on building a business your way.

6. **"Small Giants"** by *Bo Burlingham*
   — A deep dive into companies that chose to be great instead of big, highlighting sustainable, values-driven growth.

About the Author

Elvis Gboji Ajai is an entrepreneur, builder, and advocate for practical, scalable innovation. With a rich background in launching and scaling ventures across multiple sectors including fintech, Elvis brings a hands-on approach to business. His journey is marked not just by success, but by a commitment to learning and empowering others along the way.

Known for his ability to translate complex entrepreneurial challenges into actionable insights, Elvis has become a respected voice among emerging business leaders. The Intricacies of Small-Scale Business reflects his mission to support the next generation of builders who dare to start small and dream big.

www.ingramcontent.com/pod-product-compliance
Lightning Source LLC
LaVergne TN
LVHW092007090526
838202LV00001B/31